WRESTLING WITH THE FUTURE
Our Genes and Our Choices

WRESTLING WITH THE FUTURE
Our Genes and Our Choices

——————■——————

Committee on Medical Ethics
Episcopal Diocese of Washington
Episcopal Church House
Mount Saint Alban
Washington, D.C. 20016

Committee members who developed this report:

Cynthia B. Cohen, Ph.D., J.D., Chair
The Rev. Joan Beilstein
Barbara Bowles Biesecker, M.S.
The Rt. Rev. Theodore Daniels
Evan Gaines DeRenzo, Ph.D.
Peggy Eastman
Wendy J. Fibison, R.N., Ph.D.
Carol Lee Hilewick, Ph.D.
The Hon. Noel Anketell Kramer, J.D.
Elizabeth A. Luck, M.D.
James H. Marchbank
James L. Mills, M.D.
Judith W. Smith, Ph.D.
Karen Roberts Turner, M.A., J.D.

MOREHOUSE PUBLISHING

Copyright © 1998 by The Committee on Medical Ethics,
Episcopal Diocese of Washington

Morehouse Publishing
P.O. Box 1321
Harrisburg, PA 17105

Morehouse Publishing is a division of the Morehouse Group.

Cover art: DNA Rendering by Michael Agliolo/International Stock

Cover design by Corey Kent

Library of Congress Cataloging-in-Publication Data

Episcopal Church. Diocese of Washington. Committee on Medical Ethics.
    Wrestling with the future / Committee on Medical Ethics, Episcopal
Diocese of Washington.
        p.   cm.
    Includes bibliographical references (p. 125).
    ISBN 0-8192-1762-X (pbk.)
    1. Human chromosome abnormalities—Diagnosis—Religious aspects—
Episcopal Church. 2. Human chromosome abnormalities—Diagnosis—
Moral and ethical aspects. I. Title.
RB155.6.E65 1998
174'.2—dc21   98-27039
                                                                   CIP

Printed in the United States of America

Contents

Acknowledgments vii

Introduction 1

A. Genes and Genetic Testing 5

1. What are genes and what do they tell us?
2. What role does heredity play in the development of genetic diseases?
3. How do gene mutations occur?
4. What is genetic testing and how is it done?
5. For what genetic conditions can we test for now and might in the future?

B. The Anglican Tradition and Genetic Testing 11

1. What do we mean by the Anglican tradition?
2. What personal, ethical, and theological questions are raised by genetic testing for Anglicans and those of other theistic traditions?
3. Are there Anglican beliefs and moral teachings that respond to such questions?
4. What does the Anglican tradition say about the morality of seeking information about our genes?

C. Genetic Testing of Adults 19

1. How could genetic testing affect you?
2. How could genetic testing affect your family?
3. How could your genetic testing results be used by others in ways that would be detrimental to you and your family?
4. How can you obtain personal counseling about genetic testing?
5. How might you respond to test results?
6. Cases for study and discussion about testing adults

D. Testing Newborns, Young Children, and Adolescents **49**

1. Testing newborns
2. Testing children
3. Testing adolescents
4. Cases for study and discussion about testing children and adolescents

E. Whether to Conceive a Child **67**

1. Genetics and reasons for considering not having children
2. Making the decision
3. Case for study and discussion about whether to conceive a child

F. Prenatal Testing **75**

1. About prenatal testing
2. Making the decision
3. The morality of abortion for genetic reasons
4. Addressing the results of prenatal testing
5. Cases for study and discussion about prenatal testing

Appendixes **109**

Appendix 1. Resources
Appendix 2. Relevant Resolutions Adopted by the General Convention of the Episcopal Church

Bibliography **125**

Committee Members Who Developed This Report **129**

Acknowledgments

We thank the following individuals for reviewing either portions of this book or the entire manuscript, and for providing extremely helpful comments.

Lora D. Baum, Ph.D., Psychiatric Medicine, University of Virginia Cancer Center, Charlottesville, Virginia

Richard Beatty, B.L., law firm of Shaw, Pittman, Potts, and Trowbridge, Washington, D.C.

The Rev. Dr. John E. Booty, historiographer of the Episcopal Church, Center Sandwich, New Hampshire

Philip Boyle, Ph.D., The Park Ridge Center for the Study of Health, Faith, and Ethics, Chicago, Illinois

Ellen Wright Clayton, M.D., J.D., Pediatrics, Children's Hospital of Vanderbilt University Medical Center, Nashville, Tennessee

The Rev. Dr. Ronald S. Cole-Turner, Pittsburgh Theological Seminary, Pittsburgh, Pennsylvania

Francis Collins, M.D., Ph.D., director, National Human Genome Research Institute, National Institutes of Health, Bethesda, Maryland

The Rev. Dr. Walter V. L. Eversley, Virginia Theological Seminary, Alexandria, Virginia

Margaret A. Farley, Ph.D., Divinity School, Yale University, New Haven, Connecticut

John C. Fletcher, Ph.D., emeritus director, Center for Bioethics, University of Virginia Medical Center, Charlottesville, Virginia

The Rev. Sharline Fulton, St. Martin-in-the-Fields Church, Chestnut Hill, Pennsylvania

The Rev. Dr. Katherine Grieb, Virginia Theological Seminary, Alexandria, Virginia

The Rt. Rev. Ronald H. Haines, bishop of Washington, Washington D.C.

The Rev. Dr. Jan C. Heller, Center for Ethics in Health Care, Atlanta, Georgia

T. Patrick Hill, research scholar, The Park Ridge Center for the Study of Health, Faith, and Ethics, Chicago, Illinois

Eric T. Juengst, Ph.D., Center for Biomedical Ethics, School of Medicine, Case Western Reserve University, Cleveland, Ohio

Elizabeth Leland, economist, Burke, Virginia

The Rev. Dr. E.F. Michael Morgan, rector, Church of the Good Shepherd, Athens, Ohio

Jane H. Mullins, Swarthmore, Pennsylvania

Patricia Petrash, M.S.W., clinical social worker, Chevy Chase, Maryland

The Rev. Dr. Charles Price, emeritus, Virginia Theological Seminary, Alexandria, Virginia

The Rev. Dr. David A. Scott, Virginia Theological Seminary, Alexandria, Virginia

Timothy Sedgwick, Ph.D., Virginia Theological Seminary, Alexandria, Virginia

David H. Smith, Ph.D., The Poynter Center for the Study of Ethics and American Institutions, Indiana University, Bloomington, Indiana

The Rev. Dr. Harmon L. Smith, Divinity School, Duke University, Durham, North Carolina

The Rt. Rev. Stephen Sykes, bishop of Ely, Cambridge, England

The Very Rev. P. Linwood Urban, chair and professor emeritus, Department of Religion, Swarthmore College, Swarthmore, Pennsylvania

Ann C. Urban, M.S.W., Swarthmore, Pennsylvania

Robert M. Veatch, Ph.D., Kennedy Institute of Ethics, Georgetown University, Washington, D.C.

Allen Verhey, Ph.D., Department of Religion, Hope College, Holland, Michigan

Sondra E. Wheeler, Ph.D., Wesley Theological Seminary, Washington, D.C.

Ann Yarborough, M.T.S., Arlington, Virginia

We would also like to thank Elizabeth McCloskey, M.T.S., Brenda Gleason, M.A., Patricia Timberlake, and the Rev. George Timberlake not only for their editorial assistance, but also for their observations and ideas, which helped immensely in developing the structure and substance of this book. Of course, the Committee on Medical Ethics of the Episcopal Diocese of Washington is responsible for the final version of the material presented here; our reviewers and editorial assistants do not necessarily endorse all of our views. ∎

Introduction

What if we could glimpse into our future? Would we want to know what we might find there? Whether we should be tested for a genetic disease and perhaps learn what the future might hold in store is becoming a real question for more and more of us. Scientists are discovering gene mutations related to specific diseases at a rapid pace, and are creating techniques to test for them almost as quickly. Indeed, some experts predict that in a few years each of us will receive a genetic "report card" developed from a simple blood sample dropped onto a silicon chip. This will reveal which of many possible genetic conditions we already have, which we stand a chance of developing in the future, and which our children might inherit. Eventually, testing for genetic conditions will become so widely available that each of us may someday have to wrestle with the question, "Should I undergo genetic testing?"

Information derived from genetic tests can be both welcome and disturbing. It can tell us whether we will possibly or even definitely develop a serious disease. It can inform us about whether we might pass along to our children an altered gene for a certain disease. Testing, however, is not treatment. Because there are many gaps in scientific knowledge about genes, few treatments are available today for genetic conditions. Those of us who are tested, therefore, might receive results that we could not put to good use—and this could create a heavy emotional burden for us. Moreover, the knowledge that we gain from genetic testing could raise difficult personal questions, as well as troubling family and social questions. Clearly, genetic testing is not a procedure to be entered into lightly.

1

Genetic testing also raises significant theological questions for Christians. Does this technology give us a dangerous sort of knowledge that God does not intend us to have because we might misuse it? Or does it offer us vital information that we can apply to assist God in repairing those parts of creation that have gone awry? On a personal level, why has God let us have altered genes associated with serious conditions? Why doesn't God fix them? Are there some illnesses that are so severe that, as Christians, we should decide against having children who would suffer from them?

In the long run, we can use genetic testing to lessen human suffering by decreasing the occurrence of genetic diseases. Genetic testing can help us respect the image of God reflected in all humans and promote harmonious relations within families and communities. However, we can also use this technology in ways that diminish us as creatures with a God-given dignity, as when we discriminate in various ways against those who have certain gene mutations. We are called to use our ability to test for genetic conditions to meet our Christian commitment to love and serve God and our neighbors in ways that promote sharing, right relationships, and fairness.

Because the science of genetics is changing so rapidly, it is sometimes difficult for us to know what sorts of questions to ask about genetic testing. This book raises many of the questions that may occur to you. It also offers ways to find and develop answers that reflect your circumstances, your values and beliefs, and the concerns of you and your family. Moreover, it provides a broad Christian perspective on many of the personal, moral, and theological issues that genetic testing creates. It is meant to encourage wide-ranging conversation and discussion. This book was prepared by the Committee on Medical Ethics of the Episcopal Diocese of Washington, which includes people with diverse backgrounds in health care, theology, academics, the law, other disciplines, and just plain living. Committee members take diverse positions on many of the issues discussed in this book. This has led us to try to give a fair and reasoned discussion of the personal, ethical, and theological issues at stake in genetic testing.

The book is organized in six major sections:

A. Genes and Genetic Testing

B. The Anglican Tradition and Genetic Testing

C. Genetic Testing of Adults

D. Testing Newborns, Young Children, and Adolescents

E. Whether to Conceive a Child

F. Prenatal Testing

We recommend that after you read Part A and Part B, you proceed to Part C, even if you are more interested in one of the other sections. These first three parts contain basic ideas and information you will need in order to understand the other parts. The appendixes provide resources for those of you who seek additional information and assistance, as well as more detailed material of special interest. We give specific cases at the end of each section that will allow you to apply some of the ideas you find here and to gain new insights of your own.

We hope this book will assist you—Episcopalians and persons of other faiths or no faith—who are family members, clergy, health-care professionals, student groups, parish groups, theologians, ethicists, or interested persons. The Anglican moral tradition, out of which this book grows, is sensitive to the needs, concerns, and hopes of those among you who must make difficult decisions about genetic testing. It recognizes that the situations you face are complex and that you may experience uncertainty, pain, joy, and even tragedy as you make such choices. Yet the Anglican tradition also teaches that God is intimately present with us and active in creation in many ways—in our lives, Scripture, religious tradition, reason, and conscience—guiding and caring for us. God loves us profoundly, with all of our strengths and weaknesses, our physical and mental endowments and limitations. It is our hope that this book will encourage you to use your God-given abilities and resources in a prayerful and reflective way as you consider the paths open to you, putting yourself and those close to you into the arms of our compassionate and loving God. ■

A

Genes and Genetic Testing

To understand the power and purposes of genetic testing, you will find it helpful to become familiar with some basic concepts and recent developments in contemporary genetics. We provide an introductory overview of these for you here.

1. What are genes and what do they tell us?

Genes are tiny pieces of material found on chromosomes that can affect our health and our personal traits. Chromosomes, in turn, are minute threads of chemical compounds located in the nucleus of every cell. One way to understand how they work is to picture chromosomes as a book containing units of information—genes—that are like the pages of the book. The specific genes on each chromosome help to characterize each of us. They affect many of our physical features—everything from eye color to blood type. Our cells contain two sets of chromosomes, one inherited from our mother and the other from our father. Each set is made up of twenty-three chromosomes, which contain thousands of genes.

You have probably heard of DNA (deoxyribonucleic acid). DNA is the structure of nucleic acids of which chromosomes are composed. DNA exists as two long, paired strands that are tightly coiled in the chromosomes. A gene is any given segment along the DNA that carries instructions allowing a cell to perform a specific action. The sum of the DNA instructions is unique for each individual, except in the case of identical twins.

The rapid pace at which we are discovering genes and their functions has been accelerated by the Human Genome Project, an international research effort that began in 1990. One of its goals is to determine the location of all human genes. So far, more than 30,000 of the estimated 80,000 genes have been mapped. Of these, more than 1,600 have been identified as having an involvement in disease.

Single genes have been found that are associated with such conditions as Huntington's disease, a rare, fatal condition involving progressive mental and physical deterioration that usually appears between the ages of thirty and fifty, and muscular dystrophy, a sex-linked disorder characterized by progressive weakening of muscles and loss of coordination that usually leads to death by the early twenties. Investigators are also beginning to characterize more common complex diseases that are associated with several genes: heart disease, certain forms of cancer, and diabetes. Tests for many of these conditions, however, are not yet available. As the number of genetic discoveries increases, scientists will obtain valuable information about genes associated with many other conditions.

These advances are raising the real possibility that we will soon be able to undergo genetic testing to learn whether we already have a particular disease or stand a chance of developing one in the future. Moreover, they are helping us to learn whether we might pass a genetic condition to our children.

2. What role does heredity play in the development of genetic diseases?

Medical scientists have discovered that a variety of diseases are passed along to family members by means of genes. Here is how this happens. Genes come in pairs, one from each parent. The parent who has one gene mutation for what is known as a *dominant* genetic disease has that disease and a fifty-fifty chance of passing that mutation to each child. The parent who has one gene mutation for what is known as a *recessive* condition is called a carrier because he or she carries the altered gene, but doesn't have the disease. If the carrier marries someone who does not have the same gene mutation, none of their children will be affected by the disease. However, half of their children will themselves be carriers of the gene mutation. If the carrier has a child with someone who is also a carrier of the same gene mutation, there is a one-in-four chance that each of their children will actually develop the disease. The child must inherit a gene related to the same recessive disease from *both* parents in order to be at risk of that disease. For instance, cystic fibrosis is a serious condition that clogs the lungs and makes breathing and digestion difficult; only about half of those with this condition survive into their thirties. If a man with a gene mutation for cystic fibrosis marries a woman with a gene mutation for that disease, he and his wife face a one-in-four chance with each pregnancy that their child will be born with cystic fibrosis.

This is a simple version of how genetic inheritance works, meant only to give you an overview. You may find that the explanation behind the inheritance of a specific gene mutation in which you have an interest is more complex.

We all carry some genes associated with genetic disorders, even though our health may not be affected by them. For this reason it is important to realize that the predictive power of most genetic tests will be relatively weak. Having a gene mutation for some diseases, such as heart disease or cancer, may predispose you to developing them, but this does not mean that you will definitely have them. Environmental factors, by which we mean various biological, social, and psychological factors, can interact with genetic makeup in ways that may, but do not necessarily, lead to the development of a particular genetic condition.

3. How do gene mutations occur?

Genes can be changed or mutated in ways that cause certain genetic diseases and conditions. In the process of copying the three billion bits of information encoded in DNA, rare errors can creep in, causing the genes of which they are composed to change. Some of these new gene mutations originate during the lifetime of a person; others are transmitted from one generation to the next. It is not clear why these gene mutations occur, but scientists maintain that such errors may account for some of the beneficial changes of evolution. Although many of these mutations are harmless, some are connected with specific diseases and can have a serious impact on those who bear them.

4. What is genetic testing and how is it done?

Genetic testing can involve a laboratory procedure during which your DNA is examined to learn if you have a gene with the composition needed to perform its function properly. A small sample of blood is often all medical personnel need to carry out such testing. In addition to studying chromosomes or genes directly, genetic testing, in a broader sense, can include indirect biochemical tests, such as one for the presence or absence of certain key proteins that reveal gene mutations.

Through such testing, scientists can identify changes or mutations in a gene and determine if you have, or are at risk for, a certain disease or disorder. Sometimes they can do this before you have any signs or symptoms. Because all of your genes are present in most of your cells from the moment of conception, genetic testing theoretically can be done at any time in your life span.

5. For what genetic conditions can we test now and might in the future?

Currently genetic testing is not carried out as part of a routine health assessment. Usually it is offered when there is reason to believe, based on family history, that a person has a higher than usual chance of having a gene mutation associated with a specific disease. Genetic testing is also suggested when a person has symptoms characteristic of a genetic condition and there is a need to obtain a definitive diagnosis.

Tests for certain single gene mutations can tell us whether persons who have them will definitely develop the related disease during their life—in some cases early in life and in others later, depending on the disease. Testing to learn whether we will have a particular disease later in life, even though we have no symptoms for it now, is known as *presymptomatic* testing. For example, such testing can be done for Huntington's disease.

We can also test for certain single gene mutations for diseases that might, but will not necessarily, occur during a person's lifetime. This is termed *predisposition* testing. Those of us who learn through such testing that we might develop a certain disease may have different degrees of susceptibility to that disease. Whether it will actually develop depends on unknown genetic and environmental influences. For instance, the woman who tests positive for the mutation in the BRCA1 breast cancer gene will not necessarily incur breast cancer. It is estimated that at least 45 percent of those who carry this gene mutation will not develop the disease. Testing negative for the mutation, however, does not mean that a woman will be free of breast cancer, for other factors besides gene mutations affect who has it. Furthermore, medical scientists may not be able to forecast how severe the illness would be in those who test positive for a genetic predisposition, should it occur, for gene mutations do not affect everyone in the same way. A gene mutation that causes a severe disease in one person may barely affect another.

Tests are also being developed for future use that may tell us whether we might have *multifactorial* conditions. These are conditions that are associated with several mutated genes and with environmental factors. They occur more often than single mutation conditions. They include, for example, high blood pressure and rheumatoid arthritis. It is difficult to predict whether these conditions will occur in particular individuals. Tests for most multifactorial conditions are not yet available.

Couples both having a family history of a certain disease may consider testing to learn if each of them carries an altered copy of a gene for the same condition. This is known as carrier testing. (see above, Part A, section 2). If each of them were found to have the gene mutation for the same recessive condition, neither of them would be affected by that condition. Their children, however, would each have a one-in-four chance of being affected by it. An example of such a recessive condition is cystic fibrosis;

carrier testing for it is likely to be offered to all pregnant couples of Caucasian origin in the next few years.

Pregnant women can also have genetic testing carried out on the fetus they are carrying. This form of testing, known as *prenatal diagnosis*, is most often used to detect the presence of unusual chromosomal patterns or gene mutations associated with a particular genetic condition. ∎

B

The Anglican Tradition and Genetic Testing

Although this book is offered not only to those who are Episcopalian, but also to persons of all or no religious creeds, we provide a brief overview here of the Anglican tradition's approach to genetic testing. We hope this will be of interest not only to Episcopalians imbued with this tradition, but to many other readers as well.

1. What do we mean by the Anglican tradition?

The Anglican tradition refers to the teachings, practices, and customs of the Anglican Communion. This is a worldwide Christian body whose historical roots can be traced through the post-Reformation Church of England to the earliest church recorded in the New Testament. The various branches of the Anglican Communion, while independent constitutionally, are theologically and morally interdependent. The Episcopal Church in the United States is one such branch. No central governing authority mandates what individuals within the many churches in the Anglican Communion must believe or how they must act. Individuals are called to act according to their conscience, according to what they believe is right and true. The role of the church is to inform and shape conscience. The church not only provides pastoral support and prayers, but also offers teachings on issues related to important matters in the lives of individuals and the community. Thus, individuals are not left alone as they make decisions, but can share in the wisdom of the community of faith.

The faith of the Anglican Communion is grounded in Scripture, tradition, and reason, and is nourished in a sacramental structure of worship and spirituality. Anglicans are not required to subscribe to a detailed statement of doctrine. Anglicans have found sufficient the statements of belief given in the creeds that are contained and used in the context of corporate worship. The Baptismal Covenant and the catechism of the *Book of Common Prayer's* respective editions of each branch of the Anglican Communion, also express basic Anglican beliefs. The primary expectation of members of the Anglican Communion is that they join with consenting minds in the worship of God, as set out in the *Book of Common Prayer.*

2. What personal, ethical, and theological questions are raised by genetic testing for Anglicans and those of other theistic traditions?

Genetic testing can raise many personal concerns for each of us. Do I want to know whether I am at risk for having a particular genetic condition, since there is currently no treatment for it? How would I cope if I were tested and learned that I might have a serious disease? If I decide to have testing done, should I tell members of my family about the results, even if this would reveal information I would rather keep private? Wouldn't this cause them worry and apprehension? Are there compelling reasons why my children should undergo genetic testing? If a prenatal test indicates that the fetus I am carrying has a very serious condition, what decision should I make about continuing the pregnancy?

These concerns, in turn, lead to religious and theological questions. Do I have a responsibility as a Christian to have genetic testing done? How is God ordering and governing my life? Did God cause me to have a genetic disease? Are there uses of genetic testing that could go beyond the limits that we believe God has set on our intervention into the natural order? Theologians point out that our ability to carry out genetic testing raises questions that go beyond the harms and benefits of such tests for us as individuals. It also opens fundamental social and moral questions about our purpose in this world, how we are to carry out God's work in our lives, and what we owe our neighbor and our community.

3. Are there Anglican beliefs and moral teachings that respond to such questions?

Anglican moralists have embraced many traditional Christian moral principles and distinctions, but they have not set up an authoritative system of moral teachings by which to answer troubling ethical questions. Instead, they hold a traditional structured approach to moral theology in tension with individual freedom of thought. Because human nature and the situations in which humans find themselves are complex, John Habgood, a contemporary Anglican bishop, observes that morality "cannot be reduced to a single formula, but must itself be complex and must reckon with human life, not in the abstract, but in its totality. . . ." (John Habgood, "An Anglican View of the Four Principles," in *Principles of Health Care Ethics*, ed. Raanan Gillon [London: John Wiley and Sons, 1994] p. 56).

The sources of moral authority that guide ethical deliberations for Anglicans are Scripture, tradition, and reason, each informed by experience. Scripture provides a witness to the events that lie at the heart of the Christian faith and an interpretation of how a life based on that faith is lived. It also presents fundamental principles of theology and ethics. Tradition offers the accumulated and developing wisdom of the Church, its central beliefs and teachings, as it responds to the events in Scripture and the initial interpretation of them set out there. Reason is, of course, needed to interpret Scripture and tradition. We reflect upon Scripture and tradition in the light of human knowledge and experience, and reflect upon human knowledge and experience in light of Scripture and tradition. There is no single accepted way in which Anglicans move from these three major sources of moral authority to specific circumstances. How each is applied and weighed in the balance when they conflict can lead Anglicans to different conclusions about specific questions.

The basic moral framework shared by Anglicans includes the following features:

- A conviction that a moral order pervades creation and that it is grounded in God's wisdom. We can understand something of this order and perceive something of God's purposes through the gifts of reason and grace. Anglicanism acknowledges that our powers of moral reasoning are flawed and that at times we ignore this moral order and choose sinfully. Yet it also recognizes that God moves in us and calls us back to the moral life when we err.
- A perception that living a moral life is essential to our relation to God. Indeed, we share the divine life, in a sense, for as Richard Hooker, an early Anglican theologian, declared, God has "deified our nature, though not by turning it into himself, yet by making it his own inseparable habitation" (Richard Hooker, *Of the Laws of Ecclesiatical Polity* v.54.5 in the *Folger Library Edition of the Works of Richard Hooker*, W. Speed Hill, general editor, vol. 4 [Cambridge, MA: The Belknap Press of Harvard University Press, 1977]).
- The belief that the moral life is not narrowly focused on the attitudes, desires, and intentions of individuals, but has a social dimension rooted in our communion in the body of Christ. We are called by God to take seriously the values of family, church, and community, nurturing them as places where the vulnerable are protected and the stranger welcomed.
- A concern for the values of love and justice, based on the beliefs that creation is good and that each person, as a creature made in the image of God, has unique worth. Our worth is grounded in our relation to God, *not* in any specific features— including genetic features—we may possess. We are called to love one another and seek a just social order in which the dignity of each person can be recognized.

Given the flexibility and openness of this moral framework, it is not surprising to find that different Anglicans and different branches of Anglicanism sometimes express divergent views on ethical issues. Anglican moral theologian Timothy Sedgwick observes that

Differences in moral judgments are not simply or narrowly matters of right and wrong. Rather, differences in judgment reflect differences in understandings that can be articulated, respected, and debated. . . . Christian ethics and moral theology provide the basis for critical reflection that informs moral judgments and promotes respect for those who may differ ("Introduction," *The Crisis in Moral Teaching in the Episcopal Church* [Harrisburg, PA: Morehouse Publishing, 1992] p. 9).

The Anglican tradition, as Sedgwick points out, has a commitment to respect the differing views that faithful people might reach on difficult moral issues, even as it acknowledges that people of faith are not excused from responsible thought stemming from Christian belief.

This Anglican moral vision will guide us as we discuss personal, ethical, and theological issues related to genetic testing. Many of these questions are so new that they have not yet been considered fully within the Anglican or the wider religious community. Biblical and traditional writers did not have to wrestle with the challenge of discerning how God might be understood as creating life through genetic processes such as mutation and recombination. Contemporary Christian thinkers, moralists of other religious traditions, and secular ethicists offer views that will assist us as we grapple with these novel questions. An Anglican approach encourages us to seek insights from a variety of such sources, weighing them in the light of Scripture, the Christian tradition, and reason.

4. What does the Anglican tradition say about the morality of seeking information about our genes?

Some Christians think it is wrong to obtain information about our genes. They believe that our genes are so closely tied to our very nature as human beings that we endanger our God-given human status by dissecting them. These Christians reason that, since God established the natural order, the way in which our genes work should be left in God's hands. They fear that genetic testing will lead us to tinker with our genes, and this, in turn, will prompt us to usurp what is rightfully God's domain. Those who would delve into genetic codes with the hope of fixing and completing creation, they hold, would do so in presumptuous error.

A related belief of these Christian critics of genetic testing is that it is wrong to peer into "the book of life" (Exod. 32:32, Rev. 20:12), which they interpret as a book about this life, in order to get a glimpse of our future—and perhaps learn how we will die. Genetic testing promises to reveal not only whether we might develop conditions for which there could be some cure or treatment, but also whether we will experience fatal conditions for which there is no therapy. These critics maintain that God does not intend us to have this sort of knowledge. To acquire it is akin to eating the forbidden fruit in the Garden of Eden.

In responding to these concerns, Christian supporters of genetic testing observe that God not only created the world in all its richness and variety, but also continues to act within it, unfolding its varied possibilities. The same God who hung the stars in the heavens and set the planets into their orbits cares for human beings. We express our likeness to God, in part, by cooperating to shape the natural order. As stewards of creation, we are called to mend, transform, and renew the world in ways that we discern are in accord with God's purposes. Moreover, we are urged to follow the example of Jesus and compassionately to heal God's creatures. We are to use the capacities for scientific knowledge that God has given us to alter the progression of disease and to care for those who are suffering. In doing so, we glorify God and benefit humankind. As Anglican theologian Eric Mascall declared, "Christianity does not believe that God became man simply in order to bring human history to a full-stop and to reduce man to the status of a divinely certified fossil" (*Christian Theology and Natural Science* [North Haven, Connecticut: Archon Books, 1965] p. 314).

Supporters of genetic testing therefore believe that we are morally obliged to respond to genetic diseases because they create immense pain and suffering. The fruit of the tree of the knowledge of good and evil in the Garden of Eden brought to Adam and Eve a kind of comprehensive knowledge, power, and independence that rightfully belongs only to God. That is why Adam and Eve were to refrain from eating it. When they succumbed to temptation and ate of the fruit, they saw themselves in their nakedness as creatures who wanted to have equality with God. Yet we have no reason to think that genetic testing similarly invades a special domain that we are not to enter. Such testing does not change our very nature as human beings or our identity as individuals; it does not give us equality with God. Rather, it allows us to assess whether something has gone amiss with our genes, something for which we may be able to use God's gifts of medicine and science to treat. In this respect, genetic testing is no different in kind from other forms of medical testing, for it is to be used for the glory of God and the welfare of humankind.

This view is in keeping with the Anglican tradition, which has historically encouraged us to pursue knowledge and develop more accurate ways of understanding the natural order. Therefore, our committee believes that we have an obligation to respond to God's call and to develop and use genetic testing in ways that serve creation. Yet we, along with many others in the Anglican tradition, recognize that complex and troubling questions emerge regarding the appropriate applications of this technology. In our brokenness, we sometimes misuse the very gifts God has given us for our own glory, power, and wealth. C. S. Lewis has warned us that:

> Each new power won *by* man is also a power *over* man. Each advance leaves him weaker as well as stronger. In every victory, besides being the general who triumphs, he is also the prisoner who follows the triumphal car. . . . For the power of Man to make himself what he pleases means, as we have seen, the power of some men to make other men what *they* please" (*The Abolition of Man* [New York: Macmillan, 1978] pp. 71–72).

Our capacity for sin should make us cautious about our ability to become genetic engineers. We must proceed slowly and carefully in the development of genetic testing, using it for purposes that an informed conscience would accept as good.

Bishops and deputies at the 1991 General Convention of the Episcopal Church recognized this in a resolution related to genetics that they adopted (see Appendix 2). In it they maintained that it is theologically and ethically appropriate to test for genetic conditions, and to attempt to prevent or alleviate human suffering caused by genetic diseases.

Thus, our committee believes that it is morally appropriate to learn about genetic disease and to develop moral guidelines that allow genetic testing to be conducted in accord with what we discern of God's purposes. It is our hope that we can offer you who read this book new moral and theological insights as you address some of the pressing personal, ethical, and theological questions that genetic testing raises. We invite you to explore these serious issues with us in the remainder of this book. ■

C

Genetic Testing of Adults

Those who are seriously considering genetic testing ask many questions before deciding whether to proceed with it. Even if you are not currently thinking about such testing, you may want to know what sorts of questions it raises so that you can understand what is at issue, should you decide someday to undergo genetic testing.

1. How could genetic testing affect you?

If you are thinking about having genetic testing done, you may wonder, "Do I really want to know whether I might have a genetic condition?" "How would I respond if I were tested and a serious problem were found?" "What should I tell my family, friends, or employer about my test and its results?" Such questions may create considerable anxiety for you and incline you to think you'd rather not go through with genetic testing procedures. Before making a decision one way or another, you may want to seek answers to the following basic questions.

a. Why might you have genetic testing done?

There are a number of reasons why you might consider having genetic testing done. Many are related to your family history or to certain symptoms you may be experiencing. These reasons include:

- To learn whether you are currently affected by a genetic condition;
- To learn whether you will definitely be affected by a genetic condition in the future;

- To learn whether there is some probability that you will be affected by a genetic condition in the future;
- To learn whether you might pass mutations for a genetic condition on to your children;
- To learn whether the fetus you are carrying is affected by a genetic condition.

Genetic testing is unlike most other medical tests, for it can offer you information not just about you, but also about others in your family and about your children. Thus, it raises questions about your obligations to others. It may also provide you with news about which you can do nothing, raising the question of whether the information you learn is of value. Because of such features, genetic testing has the potential to create benefits and burdens you will undoubtedly want to weigh in light of your significant values and beliefs. Yet you face decisions about genetic testing not simply as a utilitarian calculator of benefits and burdens, but as a person created to trust God and to live according to the values of Christianity. Thus, Anglican readers will be especially drawn to assess these benefits and burdens in view of the moral framework outlined in Part B, particularly in terms of their commitment to love and be just to others.

b. What are some of the benefits of genetic testing?

Although each person's situation is different, there are some commonly accepted benefits of this testing that you may wish to take into account. Genetic testing may:

- *Relieve your anxiety.* Your anxiety and the worries of those close to you will undoubtedly lessen should you learn you don't have a gene mutation associated with a serious condition.
- *Reduce your uncertainty.* If your family history suggests that you are at risk of developing a serious genetic condition, you may be unsure of your future health status and that of your children. Genetic testing may help decrease some of your uncertainty, even if it indicates that you do have the condition of concern. Some people find this to be a great benefit of genetic testing.
- *Eliminate the need for further testing or screening.* If you do not have the genetic mutation for which you have been tested,

you will not have to undergo frequent tests (some of which are invasive) and checkups that you might otherwise have had to experience in order to learn if you were developing the suspected condition. If it is found that you are not a carrier of a gene mutation, you will be able to avoid medical screening for the disease of concern.

• *Lead you to investigate possible treatment.* Should test results indicate that you do have a gene mutation associated with a genetic disease, this may spur you to look into whether there is or soon will be a treatment to lessen the severity of the condition, eliminate it, or prevent it entirely. You should know, however, that at this time there are very few effective treatments or cures for the majority of genetic diseases. There is hope, though, that some may be available in the future.

• *Assist you in making decisions about the future.* Another potential benefit of genetic testing is that it will give you the opportunity to take an informed role in maintaining your health. You may want to have more frequent checkups so that treatment, if any, can begin as early as possible after diagnosis. Having information from the test can assist you in making more realistic decisions now and in the future. For instance, knowing that you may have certain symptoms and need specific sorts of help and education in the future could prompt you to make important decisions about your life better made now than later. You can choose to live life in a mindful, joyful manner, fully engaging today in what is possible for you.

• *Inform your decisions about having children.* Genetic testing may indicate whether you might pass altered genes for a certain condition on to your children. Having this knowledge can assist you in making difficult decisions about childbearing.

• *Draw your family closer together.* Although you may receive disturbing test results, you may find that your family pulls closer together in response and that members are eager to assist you in new and supportive ways.

c. What are some of the burdens of genetic testing?

There are also some burdens of genetic testing that you will want to consider in view of the values and beliefs by which you lead your life. Genetic testing may:

• *Heighten your anxiety or depression.* If you receive results that suggest you have a gene mutation associated with a serious condition, you are bound to experience stress and anxiety. The emotional impact of learning this information might lead you to change your plans for the future in ways that are not in your best interests. Stress and anxiety might cause you to feel pessimistic about the future, and contribute to feelings of powerlessness. They might also lead you to think less of yourself as a person.

• *Be difficult to interpret.* Genetic test results can be ambiguous. Not everyone who has a certain gene mutation associated with a disease will definitely have that condition. Some do and some don't. Thus, tests may not confirm or deny whether you will have a serious disease or condition, but indicate only that this is a possibility. Moreover, genetic tests may not reveal how severe the symptoms of a certain condition would be. A genetic disorder that creates only mild difficulties for some individuals might cause serious ones for others. Therefore, testing may not be as predictive as you would like.

• *Create uncertainty.* If you learn that you are predisposed to a genetic disease but don't know whether you will have it, you may find it difficult to wrestle with the resulting uncertainty. If you know you will have a certain condition but don't know how severe it will be, you and your family may face considerable uncertainty and additional anguish.

• *Impair your planning for the future.* Coping with this burden could be difficult, and might cause you to become discouraged about planning and moving ahead with your life.

• *Expose you to discrimination in insurance and employment.* Another disadvantage of genetic testing is related to how the resulting information might be used. If tests reveal that you are, might be, or will be affected by a genetic condition, such results might cause discrimination in employment and health-care insurance. Results of genetic tests have been used by some health insurance companies to limit the coverage they provide or to increase the premiums of those found to have a gene mutation. Furthermore, employers are sometimes wary about hiring or keeping people who have genetic disorders, or who might have them in the future (see below, Part C, section 3).

• *Strain family relationships.* Test results that show you have a gene mutation can cause strained relationships within your family for a variety of reasons. For instance, other family members may now fear that they are also affected, and may resent that your test results have raised this possibility for them. A rift could be created if some family members want the results of genetic testing and others do not.

d. As you weigh the benefits and burdens of genetic testing, what questions could you discuss with your doctor and other health-care professionals?

The benefits and burdens of genetic testing cited above closely parallel each other. Thus, while testing may create anxiety in some people, it may lessen anxiety in others. You will want to weigh these benefits and burdens in light of your particular situation and your deeply held values and beliefs. To get a better sense of what is medically and personally at issue, you will probably want to discuss with health-care professionals some of the following questions, along with others you may have, before you have any testing done:

• How is the test done? Is it risky? Is it painful?

• How reliable is the test? Are the testing procedures still part of a research project, or have they entered into clinical practice?

• How many conditions can be tested for with one blood sample?

• How expensive is the test? Will my health-care insurance cover it?

• How serious is the disease or condition for which I might be tested? What are its symptoms?

• Would the test indicate that the disease of concern will definitely occur, or that it might possibly occur? If the latter, how likely it is that I would eventually be affected?

• Are there any effective treatments for the condition? If so, how burdensome are they? Are they experimental?

- How expensive could treatments for this condition be? Would my health-care insurance cover them?

- How might my test results affect other members of my family and the children I have or might have in the future?

- Will the test results be kept confidential? What can be done to protect their confidentiality ?

- Could the information derived from the test affect my health-insurance coverage? My job?

- What sort of counseling would be available to me before I decide to have the test? Would counseling be available to me after the test?

- Are there support groups and patients who could provide me with information and assistance? (See Appendix 1.)

e. What obligations have those administering the genetic tests to inform you about your choices?

In their professional codes of ethics, health-care givers express the belief familiar to Christians: Each person has unique worth. This obligates them to gain your informed consent before they carry out any testing procedures for or on you. The information they offer as you are deciding whether to be tested should be balanced, accurate, and up-to-date. Moreover, health-care professionals should be supportive and aware of your questions and concerns.

f. Will you be able to understand the information health-care professionals give you?

Genetic information can be complex and therefore easy to misunderstand. If you are having trouble with it, ask your caregiver to explain it to you in simpler terms. You should not be embarrassed to ask your health-care professionals to repeat information that you do not understand.

g. Do you really want to know whether you have a genetic disease? Would it be wrong for you not to be tested?

All of us, when faced with the possibility of receiving discouraging news about our health, are inclined to draw back and think, Maybe I'd rather not know about this. You will want to consider whether you have good reason to obtain the information genetic tests might reveal or whether you are properly hesitant about doing so.

Your concerns may be well-founded. Perhaps your family history indicates that you might have a genetic condition for which no treatment is available. Testing for it, therefore, might seem pointless and burdensome to you. Perhaps you feel that even if treatment were available for the condition, it would be too difficult for you to undergo. If so, you might prefer not to receive a diagnosis that puts pressure on you to have that treatment.

Yet there may be good reasons for you to have genetic testing done. Should the test indicate you have a genetic condition, it could prompt you to make important decisions about your life that are better made now than later. Moreover, if you choose not to be tested, you might always wonder whether you could have used the test results in a way that would have had a positive effect on you and on those you love.

Within the Anglican tradition there is no absolute answer that will tell you whether it would be right or wrong for you to decide not to be tested. This depends on what genetic condition is involved and how serious it is, your particular circumstances, who else would be affected, and many other factors. Look over the benefits and burdens of such testing, described above, and look over the discussion of those values important to the Anglican tradition (see above, Part B). Ask those who would do the testing the questions suggested above. Then read the sections that follow. Talk over your concerns with those you trust—your priest, your family, and good friends (see below, Part C, section 4). You may also want to ask God what you should do in these circumstances.

h. If your family history suggests that you are at risk of a serious disease in the future, should you be tested for it?

If you are thinking about being tested for a disease that might develop in the future, it might seem difficult for you to know about it far in advance. Some people believe they would find the burden of knowing about it too uncomfortable, and therefore elect not to be tested. Others want to know as much as possible about what the future might hold for them, no matter how terrible, and they choose to have testing done.

You face a difficult personal decision, and either choice can bring some anxiety with it. If you choose to be tested and learn that you have the genetic alteration of concern, you will worry about your future and that of your family. But should you decide not to be tested, you may also have anxiety, for you may wonder what testing might have revealed. A major factor affecting your decision to be tested may be whether or not there is any effective treatment for the condition in question. If preventive steps are available or measures exist that lessen the severity of the illness, testing could be beneficial to you. But if there is nothing that can be done to avoid developing the condition or to treat it when it occurs, testing may not be of any use and may produce some burdens for you.

In deciding what to do, you will undoubtedly want to take not only your needs but also those of your family into account. Will some of them also be affected by a disease later in life if tests reveal that you will be? If so, should they know? Even if they don't stand a chance of having the condition themselves, might it be important for them to know about your possible future condition so that they can be of assistance to you?

You may have appropriate reasons for deciding not to be tested in these circumstances. It would be right to decide against it if you can find no benefits that override the burdens testing would place on you and your family. Before you make a decision about whether to be tested, you will find it useful to get help in considering all the issues involved. What does the Anglican concern for the values of love and justice call you to choose in these circumstances? Clergy and pastoral counselors can assist you in thinking through the moral and theological implications of either decision. You will want to pray for guidance before you decide. A loving and compassionate God will provide you with strength and support as you make this decision.

2. How could genetic testing affect your family?

a. Why do you need to take your family into account in deciding whether to be tested?

If the condition for which you might be tested runs in families, the choices that you make about being tested will also have significance for the rest of your family. For this reason, genetics, perhaps more than any other area of medicine, challenges us as Christians to look beyond our own health-care needs to those of others. Each of us, while created a unique individual, is also formed by God in such a way that we cannot live in isolation. We grow and develop our identities in relationship with others. The possibility that genetic testing of one family member will have an impact on others reminds us that we are called to exercise our God-given freedom of choice responsibly and with love of our neighbor—in this case, our family.

b. Should you discuss with your family your thoughts about whether to be tested?

It is advisable that you talk with your family about the possibility that you will have genetic testing done when the following circumstances apply.

When others in your family might be affected by your test results, it is important to discuss with them the possibility that you will have genetic testing done. Should test results indicate that others in your family have a genetic disease or are susceptible to one, disclosure of this information could provide them with the opportunity to give greater attention to their own health care.

Second, if you are a carrier for a condition that might affect your children, you should let others in your family know (see above, Part A). Your brothers and sisters might also be carriers, and their children could be affected. The information you give them might influence their future reproductive decisions. The Anglican belief that our moral life has a social dimension that is grounded in our unity in Christ informs your decision here.

Third, it might be necessary to test other members of your family in order to confirm your own diagnosis. This would require that you talk with them about your own testing decision.

Finally, test results might reveal certain information about family members that they want to keep private, for example, that a child's rearing parent is not his or her biological parent. Those family members involved would want to prepare for the disclosure of such emotionally sensitive information (see below, Part C, section f).

c. Won't this be hard for all of you? Wouldn't it be better not to tell them that you're thinking about being tested?

Discussing with family members the possibility of your undergoing genetic testing can be difficult for everyone. You may be worried that if you are tested and learn that you have the genetic mutation at issue, others in your family who are tested and don't have it may feel guilty. You may think that if you have the genetic alteration, your parents will blame themselves and believe that they are responsible for having given you an illness.

Even though such concerns may make it difficult for you to discuss genetic testing with your family, your underlying love and concern for them and your responsibilities as a Christian will indicate, in almost all cases, that you should talk with them about it. They, too, may have important health issues at stake. Furthermore, many families want to provide their members with loving support to help them get through a difficult testing period.

d. Should you tell your fiancé or spouse that you might be tested?

Special questions about genetic testing arise in relation to the person with whom you plan to share the rest of your life. In the marriage ceremony in the *Book of Common Prayer*, husbands and wives promise to love, comfort, honor, and keep each other in sickness and in health (p. 424). These promises create special obligations for you and your spouse. To fulfill them, you should speak openly with your spouse or spouse-to-be about the possibility of having genetic testing done.

If genetic testing might reveal that you are likely to develop a serious, disabling disease, you have an obligation as a Christian to reveal this to the person with whom you share or will share your life. If testing information would bear on your joint decision about having children, it is morally important to disclose to your fiancé or spouse the possibility that you will be tested. Although broaching this subject with the person you love raises the tragic possibility that he or she may decide not to continue your engagement or marriage should you have the gene of concern, it also avoids the possibility that your relationship may be adversely affected by the resentment he or she would undoubtedly feel once the information leaks out about not having been told.

e. Aren't there some in your family who might be harmed if you are tested?

If you are convinced that talking about the possibility of your having genetic testing would create substantial harm to a particular family member, and if others who know about your family circumstances and have sound judgment agree, then it would be acceptable not to tell that person. It is especially important to talk with a priest or pastoral counselor to gain sound moral advice in such situations. Your relative's health or that of his or her children may be at risk due to an inherited genetic condition or predisposition. You will want to be thoroughly convinced that it is best to keep your relative unaware of this.

f. Could genetic testing reveal family secrets?

Genetic testing can uncover information that families have chosen to keep hidden. For instance, it could reveal that one of a child's parents is not his or her biological parent or that a child has been adopted. Disclosing such secrets could cause discord and distress within a family. When testing indicates that the rearing father is not the biological father of a child, this might, in rare circumstances, put the mother in danger of being physically abused by a deeply hurt husband. Because of this, a commission of the Institute of Medicine of the National Academy of Sciences recommended that if genetic testing shows that a child's biological father is not the rearing father, the genetic counselor should not give this information to the rearing father if he is unaware of it. Instead, it should be left up to the child's mother to decide whether to tell him. However, the commission recommended that even if paternity is kept a secret, both partners should be given accurate information about any genetic risks to a child that are discovered during testing, for the sake of the child. This is consonant with a Christian approach to this difficult matter, for it is morally responsible to protect the mother from serious physical or emotional harm, and yet to safeguard the health of the child. Therefore, we believe it is in keeping with the Christian tradition to adopt the Institute of Medicine's recommendation.

g. What sorts of questions should you discuss with your religious counselor or a genetics professional, as appropriate, about the impact of testing on your family before you speak with your relatives?

You may want to discuss some of the following questions:

- What benefits would there be for my family if I were to have genetic testing done?

- Could my testing be burdensome for my family?

- Would members of my family have to be tested in connection with my test? Would young children in my family have to be tested?

- How has such genetic information affected relationships within other families? How might it affect those in my family?

3. How could your genetic testing results be used by others in ways that would be detrimental to you and your family?

a. What is "genetic discrimination"?

Firing or refusing to hire those who are at risk of genetic disease or refusing to give them health-care insurance is called *genetic discrimination*. This involves negative treatment of a person on the basis of genetic testing results, even when that person shows no symptoms of illness. In the 1970s, some African-Americans who were found to be carriers of a mutation for sickle-cell anemia were denied employment even though they were healthy and would never develop the disease. Such genetic discrimination might occur today, for instance, if an employer refused to hire or promote an employee whose genetic profile revealed that he or she had a likelihood of contracting an incurable and debilitating disease in the future. The employer might conclude that the employee's shortened number of work years and potentially significant medical expenses presented unacceptable costs to the business. The few studies carried out on this issue suggest that there is not a widespread problem of genetic discrimination in the United States. Yet it is a matter of concern.

b. Would your test results be kept confidential?

The principle of confidentiality means that private information about you should not be disclosed to others. Health-care professionals have a duty of confidentiality regarding knowledge they obtain about you as a patient. Consequently, you have reason to expect that information you give to those who test you, or information they learn from testing you, will not be given to others without your permission. Courts and legislatures throughout the country have generally acknowledged the duty of confidentiality and have incorporated it into the law. Some recognize an exception to the rule of confidentiality, however, in circumstances when keeping information about a person private would create a credible threat of serious bodily harm to someone else.

You waive your right to confidentiality if you consent to the disclosure of information about yourself to others by those who are carrying out genetic testing or by the doctor who receives your test results. This waiver means they can give medical information about you to others. When you sign a form authorizing others, such as health- or life-insurance companies, to obtain copies of your medical records from those carrying out testing or from the doctor who receives test results, you are allowing these professionals to disclose your test results to these third parties.

There are times when you may be required to release details of your medical records whether you want to or not, or when your doctor may be required to do so without your consent. For example, when you apply for a health- or life-insurance policy, you or your physician may be required to disclose certain genetic information about you so that you can be considered for insurance. After you have insurance coverage, you may be required to disclose your genetic test results to your insurer if you want to obtain payment for those tests and for any further treatments.

The law does not currently prohibit these required disclosures because it considers getting insurance to be a voluntary business arrangement. Some argue that such information may be needed by the insurance company to assess its risk of insuring you or to establish the cost of your policy premiums.

c. Could you be denied insurance because of your genetic test results or those of family members?

In some circumstances, insurers will have access to all the genetic information about you that is available. Some suggest that this may put you at risk of losing your health-care insurance or of being denied coverage altogether. Some insurers have been known to refuse to cover, or to drop from coverage, those at high risk for certain genetic conditions. People who are not sick, but who have a known genetic condition in their family, also have been refused health-insurance coverage. The insurers involved make these decisions in order to cut their costs and lower the prices of their premiums. If this might happen to you, you may want to consider avoiding genetic testing.

d. Could you be denied employment because of your genetic test results or those of family members?

Employers can gain a great deal of information about the genetic status of job applicants and employees. If you are applying for a job, a preemployment health-care checkup may reveal your genetic testing results to a prospective employer. As genetic testing becomes more routine and less expensive, it may become a regular part of any employment-related physical examination that you must take. Since employers are not necessarily required to reveal the results of these examinations, a prospective employer could know more about your genetic profile than you do.

If you are employed and you file a claim for an insurance payment, you may find that medical information supporting that claim is channeled through your employer. An increasing number of employers are providing their own health-care insurance to their employees. If this is true in your case, it increases the likelihood that your employer will gain genetic information about you. Employers can not only learn about your genetic status, but also about that of your family members who are covered by the same insurance policy.

There is little data available on whether genetic discrimination in employment is occurring on a large scale. Some believe that genetic discrimination in employment is not a frequent problem, whereas others hold that it is widespread. Still, there is cause for concern. For instance, employers may refuse to hire individuals for positions such as train engineers or pilots if they are found to have a genetic predisposition to heart disease or Alzheimer's disease. It is argued that they might endanger public safety. Or, an employer might be concerned that an employee who is likely to contract a debilitating genetic disease might have significant medical expenses and fewer work years. Such an employee might represent unacceptably high costs to the employer and may be fired. The potential for high employee bills might be a concern if the employer is self-insured and if the costs of covering certain illnesses could cripple the business. The other side of this problem is *job lock*, where an employee dares not leave a job that has adequate health insurance for fear of not being able to get insurance in another job. You should consider these possibilities carefully before you decide whether to be tested.

e. How might the possibility of genetic discrimination affect your decision about whether to be tested?

As people become aware that they might be refused health-insurance coverage, or charged higher insurance premiums, on the basis of their genetic test results, they might decide not to undergo genetic testing. Yet this may be detrimental to them, particularly if they could benefit from genetic testing and counseling.

This is a concern for all of us, not just for those who have reason to think they are at risk. Dr. Francis Collins, the head of the Human Genome Project, points out that we all have some deleterious genes. "We are all walking around with four or five genes that are really spoiled, and another ten or twenty or more that are moderately altered in a way that is not good for us. There are no perfect specimens" (Francis S. Collins, "The Human Genome Project" in *Genetic Ethics: Do the Ends Justify the Genes?*

ed. John F. Kilner, Rebecca D. Pentz, and Frank E. Young [Grand Rapids, Michigan: William B. Eerdmans Publishing, 1997], pp. 95-103 at 100). This means that we could all be targets for discrimination based on our genes. Recognition of the vulnerability of each of us to genetic mutations and conditions should lead us as a society to work toward eliminating whatever genetic discrimination may exist in health insurance and the workplace. The Anglican emphasis on the values of love and justice call us to work toward this end.

f. Has the Episcopal Church taken a stance on the problem of genetic discrimination?

In 1991, the General Convention of the Episcopal Church declared that "the use of results of genetic screening of adults, newborns and the unborn for the purpose of discrimination in employment and insurance is unacceptable" (Resolution A095).

g. Are there any laws that protect people with genetic conditions from genetic discrimination?

Until recently, there was little that those who found they had a gene mutation for a condition, or a predisposition to one, could do to avoid genetic discrimination. However, the Americans with Disabilities Act (ADA), which was passed by Congress in 1991, protects those who have disabilities from discrimination in employment and certain other areas. This law has been interpreted by the Equal Employment Opportunities Commission (EEOC), which administers this law, to cover people who have genetic diseases. Therefore, according to the EEOC, those with genetic conditions are protected by the Act from discrimination in employment. This ruling, however, has not been tested in the courts as of this writing. Furthermore, it is not clear whether the ADA covers those who do not actually have a genetic condition but only have a predisposition to one, or those with a family history of a genetic condition. Since the ADA is fairly new, legal scholars are still debating the extent of its protections.

The Health Insurance Portability and Accountability Act (also known as the Kennedy-Kassebaum health-insurance reform law), passed by Congress in 1996, created new protections from genetic discrimination for people covered by group health insurance. This law prohibits group health plans from using genetic information to deny insurance coverage to applicants or to exclude those who have preexisting medical conditions. However, it leaves many who must buy their own health insurance with no such safeguards against genetic discrimination. Moreover, it does not prevent insurers from charging higher premiums to those whom testing has indicated have a mutation associated with a genetic condition.

As of this writing, several national proposals have been made to remedy genetic discrimination. One proposal would prevent all insurers, both group and individual, from charging higher premiums based solely on a person's genetic test results. Others would move beyond the realm of insurance and also prevent employers from using genetic information against employees or from requiring genetic tests as a condition of employment. Still other proposals would spell out to whom health plans can release genetic information—employers; other health plans; life, disability and long-term care insurers—without the consent of the person who is the subject of such information.

Some states have passed laws that provide some protection against genetic discrimination in the workplace. These laws vary widely in their scope and in the protections they offer to individuals. Certain states have also enacted laws to prevent individuals from being denied health insurance on the basis of their genetic test results. These laws also prohibit the use of genetic information to charge higher rates or to limit the benefits of those who have a gene mutation. You should ask your physician, genetic counselor, or attorney about the law in your state.

Although all of these legal protections are important, the cost to those who seek to use them as a remedy for genetic discrimination can be great—not only in terms of money, but in terms of the time and psychological energy needed to pursue a legal case.

h. What can you do to protect your personal genetic information?

The fact that your genetic test results might be revealed to others raises unique concerns for you. Information obtained during testing and counseling can be sensitive for you and others in your family. To guard against disclosure of such information when you have not consented to it, you should discuss the issue of confidentiality with your health-care providers before you have any testing or counseling done.

Talk with those who will test and counsel you about how your records will be protected. Ask them some of the following questions:

- What will be done with the blood sample taken from me? Could it be added to a collection that would be used by researchers or clinicians? If so, would my name be revealed to them?

- If my sample will be stored, will it identify who I am?

- Will insurers, employers, or other third parties have access to genetic information about me? If so, will they be informed only if I have a genetic condition, or will they also be told if I have a predisposition to one that I might never get?

- How can I keep my genetic information confidential?

Your counselors' responses to these questions will enable you to understand the policies and procedures of your health-care providers concerning the disclosure of information about you. If you have doubts and concerns, express these to your health-care providers early in the testing process. Come to an agreement with them about any future disclosure of your personal genetic information *before* you proceed with testing.

4. How can you obtain personal counseling about genetic testing?

You will undoubtedly have many questions about some of the complex genetic information you receive, as well as about the personal and moral issues testing raises for you. It is not unusual to feel anxious about these issues and to have strong personal responses to the new information. Should testing reveal that you have a genetic condition or might have one in the future, you might feel grief, and even guilt. You might question what God's purposes are in allowing this to happen to you.

Several kinds of counselors besides your physician can help you to think through your situation and work through some of your questions and reactions. These include genetic counselors, members of the clergy and other pastoral counselors, psychologists, psychiatrists, and social workers. Each can play a unique, yet complementary role as you make medical and moral choices in light of the risks and benefits of testing, your personal and family goals, and your religious and ethical values.

a. Genetic counselors

Genetic counselors can offer a source of information and support for those who are considering genetic testing. These professionals have received special education to help you understand the process of testing, including its risks and its medical, social, and personal implications. They are prepared to assist individuals before and after testing. Usually genetic counselors work with physicians and other health-care providers, although some work independently. Your physician may be able to refer you to one. Trained counselors, however, are in short supply, and you may find that there isn't one who can assist you in the area where you live.

Genetic counselors can help you to understand your medical situation before you decide whether or not to be tested. They will discuss how the condition about which you are concerned would be diagnosed, its probable course, and whether treatments for it are available. You can talk with them about why your family history suggests that you may be at risk for this genetic condition and who else in your family might be affected. Genetic counselors will explore with you the risks and benefits of being tested in your circumstances, and how you might deal with test results. You can also discuss insurance and employment considerations with them. Additionally, these counselors can bring other issues you may not have thought of to your attention.

You will find that genetic counselors may be available to help you after testing as well. Should you learn that you have a gene mutation associated with a certain condition, they can assist you in reviewing your options. They can help you to explore the personal meaning you give to a genetic condition or risk, and they can help you evaluate what changes you may have to make in your life. Genetic counselors can refer you to mental-health providers if you are having serious emotional difficulties related to genetic testing. Furthermore, they can assist you in finding additional resources for information and support (see Appendix 1).

Genetic counselors do not believe it is their role to make decisions for you. Instead, it is their function to help you to consider many relevant medical, psychological, and social factors as you make your decision. They are professionally pledged to respect the religious and cultural views of clients, and not to pressure you into making decisions. Their traditional role is to give you supportive counseling that is not directive. This approach to genetic counseling may be changing today, as some argue that these counselors cannot be and should not be nondirective. That is, they believe that genetic counselors should express their personal values, making it clear to patients that they are doing so.

b. Clergy and other pastoral counselors

Members of the clergy or pastoral counselors may be able to help you gain insight into some of the moral, theological, and spiritual questions you have about whether to undergo genetic testing. Clergy are ordained ministers who have experience in providing care and support from the perspective of their religious tradition to those facing difficult personal decisions. They are usually educated, not only in ethics and theology, but also in clinical pastoral care. Pastoral counselors include both clergy and those who are not ordained but have a religious background and commitment. After special training in theology and one of the mental-health fields, and in some cases in religious ethics and psychology, they are certified as professionals who can assist those facing spiritual and personal difficulties related to illness. Some clergy and pastoral counselors have had specific education in genetics and risk evaluation, and can provide you with knowledgeable assistance as you grapple with some of your personal, moral, and religious questions about genetic testing.

You may want to ask a clergy person or pastoral counselor to sit through an especially difficult genetic counseling session with you. Or you may simply want one to share your uncertainty, to draw out your questions, to give voice to any pain you may feel, to pray with you, or to sit with you in silence before God.

Should you decide to proceed with testing and learn that you do have a genetic mutation for the suspected condition, clergy and pastoral counselors can help you to adjust to this information. You may find yourself wondering why God would allow this to happen to you. You may feel angry and bewildered about how to relate to God. Clergy and pastoral counselors can help you to work through these difficult religious and theological issues. Even if you learn that you do not have a suspected genetic mutation, you may need assistance in adjusting to the fact that you are not affected, but others in your family are. Some persons experience what is called *survivor guilt;* they feel blameworthy and uncomfortable about being free of a condition that runs in their family. Clergy and pastoral counselors can provide you with support if you experience such feelings.

Clergy and pastoral counselors are present to give you a perspective that takes into account God's purposes, as well as to offer you comfort and support. They are often familiar with resources in the community that can provide you with information and services related to genetic testing.

c. Psychologists, psychiatrists, and social workers

If you have a relationship with a mental-health professional, you can discuss with that person questions and concerns about your emotional health in relation to genetic testing. If you don't have such a relationship and are experiencing considerable stress in making the decision about whether to be tested or in accepting the results of testing, you may want to contact one.

Psychologists, psychiatrists, and some social workers are trained in the diagnosis and treatment of emotional difficulties. They can assess the psychological problems that you face and develop appropriate treatment plans. You may want to consult one of these professionals when serious issues of depression, anxiety, or hopelessness result from decisions surrounding genetic testing. You may also benefit from a therapy or peer support group with which you can share your experiences. Psychologists, psychiatrists, and social workers can refer you to additional resources as needed. For instance, if you need help in making changes in your household arrangements or in obtaining outside support or assistance, your mental-health counselor might refer you to an appropriate resource.

After counseling and discussion with family and friends, you will want to weigh the benefits and burdens of testing, as well as consider your Christian and other commitments and obligations. While you are trying to decide what you should do, you will also find it helpful to pray, to ask for the prayers of others, and to continue in the worship and fellowship of the church. Should you decide to have testing done, you may wish to consult with these counselors, family members, and friends about the results and gain further strength and support.

5. How might you respond to test results?

a. If your test results indicate you might develop a genetic condition or already have one, what steps can you take?

If you learn that you have or will have a genetic condition, you can use this information to guide your decisions about what to do now and in the future. If the condition you have can be treated, you can make arrangements for therapy and for check-ups afterward. Depending on the condition, you may want to review your financial resources and plan how you might cover future medical and other costs. When appropriate to the condition, you may want to review your reproductive options in light of this new information and talk with your spouse about whether to have children.

You can share your test information with other family members who might benefit from having it or who might be able to assist you in adjusting to it. Sharing such information can strengthen existing bonds and create new ones, although, as indicated earlier, it can also produce stresses and strains (see above, Part C, section 2). Even so, information gained from genetic testing can teach us to live each day more fully, drawing strength from our call to love God with all our heart and soul and mind and to love our neighbor as ourselves.

b. After learning you have a gene mutation associated with a serious condition, you may find yourself wondering why this has happened to you. Is God punishing you for something you've done? Couldn't God have prevented it?

During times of crisis, it is not unusual to experience feelings of confusion, anger, and guilt. Even if we have learned, as the Episcopal Church teaches in its catechism, that God is a God of love and mercy, that the world is good, and that creation is the work of a God who sustains and directs it, we may struggle with these teachings when confronted with serious illness and incapacity. Friends may assure us that God does not abandon us in times of difficulty and that God does not willfully inflict disease on us or allow us to suffer needlessly. But in the midst of our pain we may find ourselves asking, "Why did this happen to me and those I love?"

One way of responding starts with our recognition that God provides the universe with order, direction, and purpose. Psalm 148 extols God's creation, saying of the sun, moon, shining stars, and heavens that "he fixed their bounds, which cannot be passed" (v. 6). God established the parameters of the way the world unfolds and also allowed chance to play a role in its development. Chance works to some degree at the genetic level, where gene mutations can take place unpredictably. Such genetic changes have been important for the survival of human beings, for they have allowed us to adapt to new environments; if they did not occur, all human life would die when the environment changed. Thus, it may be that God permits mutations in our genes, even though some may be detrimental, for the sake of our survival and that of life on earth.

Arthur Peacocke, a noted scientist and Anglican priest and theologian, explains that the interplay of chance and order that God has built into the world fosters "the sort of complexity that we see to such a stunning degree in living organisms" (Arthur Peacocke, *Theology for a Scientific Age: Being and Becoming—Natural, Divine and Human* [Minneapolis: Fortress Press, 1993] p.

117). God brings us into a world in which order and chance create immense diversity and help us to survive.

What we know as Christians is that God loves this creation. Far from being a distant observer, God cares deeply about what happens to each of us. This loving God does not use disease as a form of punishment. Instead, God is present with those of us who learn that we are at risk of a serious condition, enfolding our anxiety and pain into God's own being, where they are transformed and redeemed by love. Thus, another scientist, and Anglican priest and theologian, John Polkinghorne, explains chance as follows:

> If love implies the acceptance of vulnerability by endowing the world with an independence which will find its way through the shuffling operations of chance rather than by rigid divine control . . . then the world that such a God creates will look very much like the one in which we live, not only in its beautiful structure but also in its evolutionary blind alleys and genetic malfunctions. (John C. Polkinghorne, *One World* [Princeton, NJ: Princeton University Press, 1986] p. 67. Quoted in Ronald Cole-Turner and Brent Waters, *Pastoral Genetics: Theology and Care at the Beginning of Life* [Cleveland: Pilgrim Press, 1996]).

c. Couldn't God intervene to fix every gene that mutates in a harmful way?

There is a great deal that we do not know about the way in which God is at work in the world. Yet we do know that God brings about healing miracles, and makes the lame walk, the blind see, and the dead return to life (Luke 7:22). Why then doesn't God, who is all-powerful, intervene in all of our suffering?

If God were to intervene continuously to "fix" genetic mutations, this would destroy the underlying order that is essential for the world to function. The predictability and regularity that nature exhibits would be severely diminished and we would be hard-pressed to know how to plan for the future. Moreover, God created the world with some degree of change and diversity inherent in it, including that brought about by genetic mutations. For God to intervene continuously to reverse such genetic mutations would violate God's intentions in the first place.

These responses cannot fully explain God's purposes in the world. Nor can they wholly soothe the spiritual chaos we may feel in the face of sickness and suffering. We know that God does not wave a magic wand and take away all suffering. And yet we also know that God is present to everyone and everything, as creator and sustainer. Above all, we know that God redeems all of life in the midst of evil, anguish, and pain. Here we stand with Jesus, even in the face of forces that cause us suffering, even if we feel abandoned, and here we trust in God. This trust calls us not to blame ourselves or one another (or God for that matter) for genetic disease and the uncertainties and certainties that it carries. In prayer we ask that God's "will be done, on earth as it is in heaven" (Matthew 6:10). This may be through physical healing, which is miraculous to our understanding, or it may be through an experience of the grace of God, who cares passionately about us. God brings healing, hope, and newness of life to us as we make the difficult and painful choices surrounding genetic testing.

6. Cases for study and discussion about testing adults

In this section we present some cases based on real situations in which people have found themselves. (We have changed the names of those involved to preserve their confidentiality.) These are designed to help you to pull together some of the considerations presented above on testing adults and to develop new insights of your own. We hope that you will not only think about them but also discuss them with others.

a. Sally's case: Testing for the gene mutation for breast cancer

Sally, who is thirty-six years old, is concerned about whether she will develop breast cancer. Her mother and grandmother both died of it. Her younger sister, Frances, was tested and found to have one of the gene mutations associated with breast cancer; Frances was recently diagnosed with the disease. Sally must now decide whether or not she should be tested for the breast cancer gene mutation.

Women with this gene mutation have a high risk of getting

breast cancer. If Sally were found to have the gene, she could take no steps to *guarantee* that she would not develop breast cancer. She could increase the number of checkups she has for it each year so that should breast cancer develop, it could be detected and treated early. She might also take medication that is currently being tested in hopes that it might prevent breast cancer. In addition, she might have both of her breasts removed surgically in an attempt to avoid the disease. However, the medical literature suggests that this does not guarantee that she would avoid breast cancer, although it does reduce the risk. Furthermore, if Sally were found to be free from the gene mutation, this would not mean that she would never have the disease. Only 5 to 10 percent of those who develop breast cancer have a breast cancer gene. So Sally might develop the disease even though she doesn't have the gene; most women who develop breast cancer have no known risk factors.

Sally is struggling to decide what she should do.

i. Should Sally be tested? Or is she better off not knowing whether she has the gene? Why?

ii. Should Sally consider the needs and interests of anyone besides herself?

iii. Where can Sally seek help as she makes her decision?

iv. If you were Sally, what would you do? Why?

b. George's case: Predictive testing for Huntington's disease

George's father recently was diagnosed with Huntington's disease, a genetic condition that becomes evident between the ages of thirty and fifty. This is a fatal condition for which no cure has been found. It leads to loss of muscular control, causing jerking movements, and to mental decline. George, who is twenty-two years old and engaged to be married, realizes that he may have inherited the gene for Huntington's disease from his father. He is torn about whether or not to be tested.

i. Has George any moral or religious obligation to be tested or not to be tested?

ii. Who should George take into account in making this decision?

iii. If George is tested and found to have the gene, should he consider never having biological children so that he will not have a chance of passing the gene along to them?

iv. To whom might George talk about this?

v. If you were George, what would you do? Why?

c. Audrey's case: Testing suggests nonpaternity

Audrey went to the assistant rector of her church for advice about a difficult decision she had to make regarding genetic testing. Her family physician had recommended that she and her husband, Fred, undergo carrier testing to help them make future reproductive decisions. The couple had two children. The first was in good health, but the other had cystic fibrosis, a serious condition that occurs when both parents are carriers of a recessive gene. Their family physician thought they should be tested now to learn whether any children they would have in the future stood a chance of having cystic fibrosis.

Audrey was reluctant to agree to the test. She had entered into a brief extramarital affair before their second child was born, and believes that the man involved is the child's biological father. If she were found to have the gene mutation for cystic fibrosis and Fred were not, this would reveal the truth. Audrey has kept this a secret from Fred. She and her minister meet to discuss what Audrey should do.

i. Why did the family physician believe it was advisable to have Audrey and Fred tested for carrier status?

ii. What harms should Audrey and her minister weigh in the balance as they discuss what she should do? Are the possible harms to Audrey alone or also to Fred and to their children?

iii. Do you think the welfare of any children that Audrey and Fred might have in the future should figure into the decision?

iv. What would you recommend to Audrey if you were her minister?

d. Ann's case: Genetic discrimination in insurance

Ann is an eight-year-old child who was diagnosed through a newborn screening program at 14 days of age as having phenylketonuria (PKU). PKU is a rare disease that can cause mental retardation. It can be prevented if a child is diagnosed at birth and put on a special diet. Ann was put on such a diet and her growth and development have been normal. Her health care costs have been covered by the company that provides group insurance for her father's employer.

Recently, Ann's father changed jobs and was told that the premium he would have to pay for his daughter's coverage under the new health-insurance plan would be three times what it was under his old one. The cost of her diet and follow-up treatment is the problem, his employer says.

   i. Should the insurance company have raised the premiums for Ann's family, even though she has no symptoms of the condition? What are the company's concerns?

   ii. If Ann had a more serious condition, could the insurance company justify raising her father's premium? Why or why not?

   iii. What options are open to Ann's father? Are there public or private resources that would help him to obtain insurance coverage for Ann?

   iv. Should we allow those who have the bad fortune of being born sick to be penalized in our society? What does the Christian tradition teach about what we owe to those who are ill? What can we do as a society to ensure that those born with genetic conditions receive appropriate health care?

e. Nancy's case: Genetic discrimination in employment

Nancy applies for a job and is offered employment with the company if she receives a favorable medical report. At the examination the company nurse obtains Nancy's consent to draw blood. When Nancy asks what tests are being performed on her blood, she is told that company policy prohibits disclosing this information. A few weeks later Ann receives a letter in the mail telling her that her conditional offer of employment has been revoked. No reason is given.

In fact, the blood test indicates that Nancy is a carrier of the gene for Duchenne muscular dystrophy. This is a sex-linked disorder characterized by progressive weakening of muscles and loss of coordination that usually leads to death by the early twenties. If Nancy has a male child, he will have a 50 percent chance of having the gene mutation for the condition. The company is concerned about the risk of higher health costs if they employ Nancy and she has a boy with muscular dystrophy.

i. Is it ethically acceptable for a potential employer to obtain medical information about an applicant without informing her of this?

ii. Does the company have a justifiable concern about keeping its health-care costs down?

iii. Should those without any symptoms of an illness be denied a job because they might have children who would incur health-care costs?

iv. How might we resolve this employment-related problem in our society? ■

D

Testing Newborns, Young Children, and Adolescents

If you are reading this section first because you are considering having your child tested, we recommend that you turn back to Parts A, B, and C to obtain basic information about genetic testing and insights into the personal and ethical questions it can raise. Then return to this section to look into special issues that can arise when testing newborns, young children, and adolescents.

Children of various ages, from birth through adolescence, can be tested for a number of genetic diseases and conditions that they might currently have or might develop in the future. In most cases, genetic testing is recommended for children only when a particular concern is present. Perhaps there is a chance that they have a condition that runs in their family, or they may display symptoms of a condition that has a genetic basis.

Within the Christian tradition, parents are viewed as stewards of their children for God. Our children are entrusted to us for safekeeping, nurturing, and growth. Thus, we have a responsibility to provide them with appropriate medical testing and treatment as needed. We are to weigh the benefits and burdens of various forms of medical tests and treatments for our children and to choose those that would offer them more benefits than burdens. When we are thinking of having genetic testing done for our children, it is important to realize that it can offer benefits to some children and families, but that the burdens of testing might outweigh its benefits for others.

1. Testing newborns

a. Why does the law require certain genetic tests for newborn infants?

All newborns must be tested for certain genetic diseases and conditions as a matter of state law. Most states require that they be tested for certain metabolic disorders, such as phenylketonuria (PKU). In some states they also must be tested for other conditions, such as sickle-cell disease, a condition that leads to anemia and shorter life expectancy. These genetic tests are required for all infants born in the state, even though a specific infant may not have a family history indicating that he or she is at increased risk for one of these illnesses. This statewide testing of all newborns for certain diseases is carried out so that those who are affected can receive early treatment and thus avoid complications. These tests are safe, accurate, and inexpensive. A few states, nonetheless, have regulations that allow parents who, because of their religious beliefs, are reluctant to have their newborns tested the option of refusing such testing.

b. Are there other genetic diseases or conditions for which some want to require testing of all newborns?

The rapid pace at which additional genes that are markers for diseases are being identified has led some to advocate testing newborns for these genes as well. Discussions are underway around the country about adding tests for genetic conditions such as cystic fibrosis (a serious condition that makes breathing and digestion difficult, and of which only about half of those diagnosed with it survive into their early twenties) and inherited forms of heart disease. Some question the usefulness of additional tests, however, arguing that such testing would provide the infants with no benefits and would unnecessarily worry parents.

2. Testing children

a. About testing

i. Why are some young children tested?

Genetic testing for young children beyond the newborn period is not usually required by law. Parents and health-care professionals, however, may decide to test children for a number of reasons.

They may choose to test children for diseases that appear during childhood because they have a family history of the disease. Or they may decide that a child should undergo genetic testing because he or she has signs of a serious childhood genetic condition, even though that condition does not appear in the family history. Health-care professionals usually will do such testing only if treatment is available for the condition of concern. For instance, children may be tested for the mutated gene (or genes) associated with cystic fibrosis or certain forms of childhood cancer because there are some forms of treatment for these conditions.

Children can also have carrier testing done to learn whether they have a mutated gene for a recessive condition that runs in their family. Information derived from such tests might give parents and other family members some insight into whether there is a chance that their future children might be affected by the condition of concern. Children who are found to have a mutated gene for a recessive genetic disease are not themselves affected by that disease (see above, Part A).

ii. Why are some health-care professionals reluctant to provide carrier testing for children?

Many health-care professionals are cautious about testing children because they don't want the results to become a burden to family members. For example, children found to have the mutated gene for a recessive disease might be labeled "sick," have lowered self-esteem, or be subjected to genetic discrimination. A child might assist another family member by undergoing what is called *linkage testing*, genetic testing that is performed to help assess whether a condition runs in a family. The child might feel proud of being able to help. Yet geneticists prefer to find other ways to diagnose that family member's condition, without testing a related child. Some health-care professionals do seem more willing, however, to provide carrier testing for a young child when this would assist parents in making a decision about conceiving another child who might be at risk of an inherited condition.

If you believe that your child would not suffer from undergoing carrier testing and, indeed, would benefit from it, you should explain this to the relevant health-care professionals and work out a satisfactory resolution of this issue.

iii. Why are many health-care professionals reluctant to test children for diseases for which there is no treatment?

Some professionals believe it can be emotionally difficult for children and their families to learn that they are at risk for a disease that they cannot take steps to prevent or treat. Families may lower their expectations for children who learn they might or will have such a condition, and the children themselves may feel as though they are somehow to blame for having the mutated gene. In addition, health-care professionals are concerned that the information derived from such testing might lead to discrimination against the children later in life, when they apply for jobs or insurance.

You may wonder, however, whether it would be beneficial to your child to be tested for a disease for which there is no treatment. Perhaps you want to know if your child is at risk for a certain condition because you believe that treatment for it could be on the horizon and you want to be prepared to use it. Or, if a genetic condition runs in your family and your child knows about it, you may believe that testing for it could alleviate the uncertainty of your child and the rest of the family, and allow you to plan for the future. If this is the way you feel, it is important to discuss this with the relevant health-care professionals and ask them to honor your request.

iv. How physically burdensome are these tests?

The tests are not usually physically burdensome. A small sample of the blood is taken and analyzed in the laboratory. Sometimes a skin sample is taken.

b. Making the decision

i. Who is responsible for deciding whether our child should be tested?

The responsibility for the decision to test a child rests with parents as stewards of their children for God. Thus, you are expected to make such judgments on behalf of your children, weighing the distinctive benefits and burdens of genetic testing in light of your perception of your child's good, and in light of other important values and beliefs. Value judgments are at the heart of such decisions, and we believe that the values of a child's parents should guide them. Health-care professionals are usually closely involved in such decisions, for they have knowledge and experience that can be very helpful. Indeed, the relationship between health-care professionals and parents often reflects a shared decision-making process in which the values of the parents play a significant role.

ii. Should your child participate in decisions about whether to have genetic testing done?

Whether your child should participate in the testing decision depends on your child's age and stage of development. Some child-development authorities maintain that even fairly young children can participate in decisions about their own health care, to a certain degree, if they can understand some of the medical information and what "risk" and "benefit" mean. Some children can carry out formal thinking by the age of eleven in that they can develop hypotheses and predict future possibilities. Having these abilities does not imply that all children of eleven years and older can make their own decisions about testing. Whether children can participate in the decision depends on their understanding of the medical facts and their ability to use reasonable thought processes.

It is important that counselors and parents talk directly to children about testing before it is done so that they understand the purpose and implications of the test. If no conversations are carried on with children, they may develop interpretations of the condition that may be unnecessarily frightening to them.

iii. What factors should you consider in deciding whether your child should be tested?

The basic question you will want to explore is whether genetic testing would offer your child certain benefits that outweigh its burdens. To determine this, you can ask questions such as the following:

- How serious is the condition in question?

  Genetic conditions vary widely in their severity—from minor ones, such as color blindness, to serious ones, such as Tay-Sachs disease, which leads to significant disability and premature death. Genetic testing is usually not performed for minor conditions, as it provides no information that is not available to you in other ways. However, testing for more serious conditions may be beneficial, depending on the answers to certain other questions (below).

- How likely is your child to get this condition?

  Some conditions for which children can be tested might, but will not definitely, occur. Testing for such conditions is known as *predisposition* testing. Whether an individual child will actually develop the disease in question depends on unknown genetic and environmental influences. Often, physicians cannot predict how serious the disease would be should it occur, since a gene may lead to serious illness in one child and yet barely affect another. Therefore, it is difficult to assess how beneficial it would be to test your child for a condition that might or might not appear.

- Is the condition likely to appear during childhood or later in life?

  When you have a family history of a genetic condition that appears in childhood and your child has symptoms that could be attributed to that condition, it is appropriate to consider having your child tested for it. However, if the disease of concern does not appear during childhood, but is an "adult-onset" condition, there may be no point in testing for it until your child becomes an adult.

  You will find that many genetic health-care professionals in genetics recommend that you put off testing your child for such an adult-onset condition until your youngster is mature enough to make an informed decision about this. Should your child have a gene mutation associated with a serious, or even fatal, adult-onset condition, these professionals fear it might be distressing to have to live with this information and yet be able to do nothing about it. Your child might feel to blame and unlovable. In addition, your child would be at risk of being labeled "sick" and of experiencing genetic discrimination now or later in life. Critics of testing children for adult-onset diseases also worry that even if your child should test negative, he or she might experience what has been called *survivor guilt*. This means that your child might feel emotional pain because he or she has escaped a condition that affects others in the family. These concerns are hypothetical, as there has not yet been much research on the impact of genetic testing on children for adult-onset conditions.

Yet you might want to test your child for an adult-onset condition if the condition at issue is serious, runs in your family, and your child knows he or she might have it later in life. Perhaps testing would relieve some of your child's uncertainty, as well as yours. You might decide, should your child learn through testing that he or she has the genetic mutation for an adult-onset condition, to plan ways in which to address the condition and create a support system that would stand your child in good stead later, when the condition does appear. You may feel that you could also help your child to develop an even deeper sense of God as one who sustains and heals, should you receive results indicating that your child might have a serious illness later in life.

You will want to take into account the considerations expressed by these professionals and your own concerns as you decide whether to have your child tested for a gene associated with an adult-onset condition. How bad is the anxiety of not knowing? How much good could be done by preparing your child for the possible condition? In the end, you must make the decision in light of your family situation and what you believe would be best for your child.

- If the condition is likely to appear during childhood, is there some early treatment for it or preventive measures that can be taken?

When treatment or preventive measures are available for a condition that appears during childhood, you have reason to consider having your child tested for it. When they are not, however, there may be no point in proceeding with testing. The benefits and burdens of testing for adult-onset conditions discussed above are also applicable here.

• Will your child understand testing information and respond appropriately to it?

You must consider your child's level of emotional, intellectual, and social maturity as you assess whether testing would be beneficial. The ability of children to understand and choose what would be beneficial to them varies, depending on the individual child, his or her age, and the testing choice at issue. If you decide to have a young child tested, you will have to help him or her understand the significance of the testing in terms that are meaningful and appropriate to him or her.

As you respond to the questions above and assess the benefits and burdens of having your child tested, you may find it helpful to turn to some of the questions raised when considering the testing of adults (see above, Part C, section 1) and to the discussion of the Anglican approach to genetic testing (see above, Part B).

iv. How might the decision you make about testing your child affect you and the rest of your family?

Should you proceed with testing and discover that your child has or might have a genetic disease, this could have a strong emotional impact on you, your child, your other children, and other relatives. Such results can be difficult to accept, especially if you are not prepared for them. It may be hard for you to understand what your child's condition involves or what the future holds for your family. You, like many parents, may feel guilty. You may become anxious and angry and may be unwilling to talk about your child's condition with your doctor or others. You and your spouse may also experience different timetables in the process of adapting, and you may find that this places stress on your marriage. In addition to these emotional issues, you might face new physical, social, and financial issues.

v. What sort of counseling is available as you decide whether to have your child tested?

If you are uncertain whether testing would benefit your child, you should discuss this question with genetic and pastoral counselors. The former can bring to the discussion specialized knowledge of genetics, experience in treating such conditions in children, and familiarity with your circumstances. The latter can assist you with personal, moral, and spiritual questions that arise for you and your child as you make your decision (see above, Part C, section 4).

c. Addressing test results

i. If you proceed with testing and learn that your child might or will have a genetic disease, how can you deal with this?

After you and your family recover from the initial shock, you will want to adapt to your new situation and move forward in your lives. Should you have difficulty coping with the news you receive, you may want to seek additional help from a psychologist, psychiatrist, or social worker. Information and support groups are available to help you learn more about the condition, how to deal with the health-care system, and how to meet social bias against children with genetic conditions (see Appendix 1).

A priest or other pastoral counselor can also help by listening to you, consoling you, and offering you insight into how God is working in your new situation. Furthermore, your parish may offer you not only spiritual and emotional support, but also practical assistance.

The difficulties that you may face as you care for a child with special needs are not to be minimized. The experience of grappling with the challenges offered by your new situation can be intimidating, but they can also be spiritually enriching. These challenges can lead you and your family to deepen your relationships with one another and with God. You may come to sense the grace of God empowering and comforting you in the midst of a daunting and yet life-giving experience.

ii. Should you tell your child about the results of testing?

If your child is old enough to be involved in the decision about testing, it is appropriate to tell him or her about the results. Consider requesting that you receive these results first so that if they indicate your child has or might have a genetic condition, you will have time to compose yourselves before you talk with your child. However, if your child is old enough to understand the significance of genetic testing, it is important not to keep him or her waiting too long after the results are available. Some parents prefer to tell their child themselves, at home. If you wish to do this, ask for advice from counselors before doing so. Of course, you need to explain test results in words that your child will understand.

If your child is too young to understand the results, you should plan to provide him or her with the information when he or she is old enough to comprehend it. Studies suggest that children with serious conditions cope better if they are told about their condition as early as possible.

Since children are concerned about how their friends will perceive them, should they have the gene of concern, it is important to discuss with them ways in which they can tell others about their condition. As counselors, Petersen and Boyd observe: "Initial feelings of being different from others quickly dissipated when friends and peers did not treat them differently than before and in fact expressed interest in the genetic testing" (Gloria M. Petersen and Patricia A. Boyd, "Gene Tests and Counseling for Colorectal Cancer Risk: Lessons from Familial Polyposis," *Journal of the National Cancer Institute Monographs*, No. 17, 1995, p. 70).

iii. If your child becomes very sick and you are having great difficulty providing him or her with appropriate care, should you consider placing your child in a care setting outside of your home?

Some unusual and serious genetic conditions may require extensive and even round-the-clock care. You may be unsure about what is best for your child—caring for him or her yourself or finding some other placement that can meet your child's needs in a kind and loving atmosphere. Some devoted parents believe that it is their duty to treat their child at home. Indeed, they may turn their home into an intensive-care unit in an effort to care for their child. Other loving parents find that they cannot meet the demands of intensive caregiving. They believe that the Christian call to love and aid others does not mean that they are required to disrupt their families to such a degree. Some parents who pour all of their energies into the care of their sick child are so exhausted that they cannot adequately care for their other children or keep their jobs. Thus, in some cases, parents may conclude that their moral responsibility for their child can be met best through an appropriate outside placement for their child. While it is extremely difficult for them to have a child they love dearly taken care of elsewhere, this decision is not unchristian. Their child's serious, long-term medical needs may be met more adequately in a facility with specially trained caregivers than at home.

Both families who care for a child with a serious condition at home and those who find a placement for their child in a qualified facility face a difficult future. Family and friends can support them in practical ways—such as occasionally providing care for other children in the family—and in emotional and spiritual ways. This is especially true for those who share a Christian commitment with them.

3. Testing adolescents

a. About testing

i. Why are some adolescents tested?

Adolescents are tested for genetic conditions for many of the same reasons that young children are tested and also for some reasons unique to persons at their stage of life. They may be tested if they have a family history of a genetic disorder and medical treatment for it is available. Adolescents may also be tested to learn whether they are at risk of a certain condition in the future for which treatment or preventive measures are available. Some adolescents are tested for adult-onset diseases, although many health-care professionals are reluctant to provide such tests for reasons explained above (see Part D, section 2).

Teenagers can also undergo carrier testing to learn whether they have a mutated gene for a recessive condition that runs in their family. Results of such tests might provide information indicating whether their children or additional children their parents might have could be affected by the condition of concern. Teenagers found to have a mutated gene for a recessive genetic disease will not have that disease themselves (see above, Part A). Health-care professionals, however, are usually reluctant to perform carrier testing on teenagers for the reasons explained above (see Part D, section 2).

Adolescents who are considering marriage or are sexually active—no matter how much their parents may have discouraged this—might also have carrier testing done in order to learn if they have a mutated gene for an inherited disease that they could pass to their children.

b. Making the decision

i. Who should make the decision whether your adolescent should be tested?

In most cases, the decision about whether your adolescent should have genetic testing carried out will be up to you as the parents. Yet, as you move toward a final decision about testing, you and your adolescent will find it helpful to share your thoughts about the matter with each other.

During adolescence children begin to develop concepts of cause and effect, right and wrong, their connection to the future, and their own mortality. Many begin to relate to God in a personal way, as well as to a community of faith. At the same time, they have a heightened concern about their self-image and frequently express the desire to have increased control over their lives. Adolescents may therefore express a wish to make their own decisions about whether to undergo genetic testing. However, studies of fourteen- and fifteen-year-olds who were asked to make medical decisions about fictionalized situations indicate that adolescents generally go along with their parents' wishes. This suggests that in most instances adolescents will be receptive to their parents' views about genetic testing and will accede to their decisions.

In considering how involved your adolescent should be in the choice about genetic testing, you will want to assess whether he or she is mature enough to cope with test results, positive or negative. Mature adolescents—those who exhibit adequate understanding of information about genetic testing, are competent, and can make choices voluntarily—can play a major role in decisions about whether they should be tested. Some experts recommend that the degree of seriousness of the condition at issue should also be a factor in determining how involved your adolescent should be in the testing decision. That is, the more serious the illness, the higher the level of maturity and competence your adolescent child should have.

Some adolescents are viewed as *emancipated minors* who can make their own medical decisions about health care and certain other matters without the involvement of their parents. Depending on the state, an adolescent is considered an emancipated minor if she is pregnant and living at home; a teenage parent, regardless of whether or not he or she is married; a college student living in a dormitory; married; or economically independent and living on his or her own. If your adolescent fits into one of these categories, he or she may be allowed to make the decision about genetic testing without your input.

Many states also recognize *mature minors*. These are youngsters who do not meet the criteria for emancipation, but are considered sufficiently mature to make decisions about their own medical treatment. Often fifteen is considered the age at which a mature minor can consent to or refuse medical treatment without his or her parents' permission. In some states, a child can be as young as twelve. Thus, an adolescent who is mature might be allowed to make an independent decision about whether to undergo genetic testing.

ii. Are there benefits that genetic testing could provide your adolescent?

Your primary question about having your adolescent tested, as was the case with younger children, will undoubtedly be whether it would benefit him or her. If the test is positive, treatment may be available for the condition. If the test brings bad news, such a test may relieve your adolescent's uncertainty and anxiety and allow your teenager to make decisions about education, career, and reproductive risks.

iii. Are there burdens that genetic testing could create for your adolescent?

The benefits of genetic testing in adolescent children must be balanced against the burdens that it can create. Many of these burdens are psychosocial. Adolescents who receive bad news from test results might feel that they are different from their friends and therefore unacceptable. Because of this, your adolescent might withdraw, interrupting the process of relating to peers that is important to his or her development at this stage. Furthermore, some parents change their ideas about their children's future prospects when they test positive for a serious disease. Some withdraw resources, such as a college education, from that child. You will want to consider whether you might limit your expectations of your adolescent if he or she should test positive.

If you consider testing your adolescent for a serious, even terminal adult-onset condition, you will naturally ask whether he or she would be devastated by a positive test result. It is difficult enough for adults to keep their balance and focus in life when they receive such results. Adolescents might have an even harder adjustment to make. Health-care professionals usually advise that adolescents wait until adulthood and then make their own decisions about whether to be tested for an adult-onset condition. If you believe that your adolescent is at a level of maturity at which he or she can deal with this information, and that it is important for your teenager to know, it would be wise to seek genetic or other counseling to help you and your adolescent make a final decision about this (see above, Part C, section 4).

c. Addressing test results

i. Should you tell your adolescent about the results of testing?

Since your adolescent was probably involved in the decision making about testing, he or she should be told about the results.

You may want to tell your adolescent the results of the test by yourself, or you may want your teen to be present with you when receiving the results from the physician who did the testing. Your rector or another church person who has worked with your adolescent might also be involved, as he or she may know your child well and recognize that your teen has special needs at this time.

If test results indicate that your teen has a gene mutation associated with a genetic condition, you will need to weigh the information and figure out how you can assist your adolescent in coping with this news. You can help your child by not denying the results of the tests. Allow your teen to experience the entire range of upsetting and conflicting feelings he or she is bound to have. Most adolescents, especially younger ones, do not tend to focus on the future, so it may be hard for your child to absorb what a test result means for him or her in one session. Let your adolescent take in what he or she is able to handle at the time. It may be necessary for you to talk about the positive result and its implications on several different occasions, taking cues from your adolescent about when to do so.

If you are concerned about how your adolescent is responding to test results, consider returning to your genetic counselor or another counselor, such as a youth minister, psychologist or psychiatrist.

ii. How can your adolescent's Christian faith serve as a resource in these circumstances?

Your adolescent's faith can provide him or her with a sense of being cared for and loved in the face of difficult medical decisions. This is a time when adolescents may discern that there is a power and strength beyond their own that upholds them. Yet it is also a time when they question God's relevance to their lives— or God's very existence. Just as adults struggle with the question of how a just God can allow suffering, adolescents may feel angry, bewildered, and doubtful of God's loving presence. One of the most significant ways we can help young people to experience God in a positive light is to allow God to work through us as vehicles of love, concern, and hope for the future. Helping your adolescent to trust God as a God of love and compassion, rather than as a God of punishment and wrath, is especially appropriate at this stage in his or her life. It is important for your adolescent to know that he or she is not alone and that God and others will not abandon him or her.

The Bible and the *Book of Common Prayer* can serve as resources to help your adolescent acknowledge the reality of his or her suffering, while at the same time nurturing a sense of hope. The Bible has many stories that speak about people faced with difficult challenges who turn to God for strength. The Psalms especially can provide comfort and encouragement as they give voice to the plaintive cry—"Where are you, my God?" and yet conclude that God is a rock and refuge. The *Book of Common Prayer* is also filled with hope about God's ability to raise us to newness of life.

Finally, a significant resource for your adolescent is a faith community, especially one in which other young people are active and involved. At church an adolescent can find the sustaining grace of the sacraments and God's word—resources necessary for strengthening and developing his or her faith in creative and life-giving ways. Participation in a caring, accepting faith community is an important way that an adolescent can nurture his or her faith in order to cope with the difficult issues that genetic knowledge can raise.

4. Cases for study and discussion about testing children and adolescents

a. The case of Fred and Lisa's children: Predictive testing of children for Huntington's disease

Fred has just received a diagnosis indicating that he has Huntington's disease. He and his wife, Lisa, are extremely disturbed by the news that he has an untreatable, progressive, fatal neurologic disease. When the doctor explains that it is inherited, Lisa asks whether their children, who are nine and thirteen years old, are at risk. The doctor tells her that each child has a fifty-fifty chance of having the condition.

Fred and Lisa decide that they must know whether the children will also have Huntington's, so they ask to have them tested for the gene mutation. The doctor points out that the disease usually does not become clinically evident until adulthood. She observes that some people do not want to know whether they will be affected and do not have testing done on themselves. Her recommendation is that the children not be tested until they are old enough to decide whether they want the information.

The question of what to tell the children about their father's illness looms for Fred and Lisa. They do not think it right to keep the children uninformed about their father's condition, for they will learn the truth eventually and will be upset about having been kept in the dark. Once they find out that they, too, might have the gene mutation, it may be very difficult for the whole family to wait until they are eighteen years old to be tested. They will have to function as a family until that time, and their family functions best, they believe, when things are out in the open. Fred and Lisa state that as parents they have the right to make the decision whether their children should be tested and that, on balance, they believe it would be wise to do so.

i. Should the children be tested for Huntington's disease? Why or why not?

ii. Does their age make a difference?

iii. Who should make the decision? Should the children be involved in making it?

iv. Where can Fred and Lisa find additional help as they make this difficult decision?

v. If the children are tested and they test positive, how much should they be told and at what age?

b. Serena's case: Adolescent sickle-cell carrier testing

A sixteen-year-old, Serena, is thinking of marrying Charles when she turns eighteen. Charles has a younger brother with sickle-cell disease, an inherited blood condition causing severe anemia and life-threatening crises. Charles has been tested for sickle-cell disease and has been informed that he is a carrier of the gene for the disease. That is, he has one gene mutation associated with sickle-cell disease and one normal gene. This means that each of his children will receive one of these two genes. If a child receives the mutated gene associated with sickle-cell disease from both parents, he or she will have the condition.

Serena wants to be tested to learn whether she, too, is a carrier. If she is and she marries Charles, each of their children would have a 25 percent chance of having sickle-cell disease. If she is not, their children will not have the condition, although they could be carriers. Serena thinks it is important for her to have this information before she decides whether to become engaged to Charles.

Her parents, however, argue that Serena does not need to know whether she is a carrier, as this will not affect her own health. If she is a carrier, she would have no increased risk of developing medical problems. But she might face discrimination if she is found to be a carrier and that becomes part of her medical record. Her parents point out that employers and insurance companies have discriminated against those who are carriers despite the fact that their health is not affected. They emphasize that this could happen to Serena, too. Furthermore, if she learns she is a carrier, she may find that Charles may not want to marry her.

i. Should Serena be tested to learn if she is a carrier? Why or why not?

ii. How should Charles figure in the decision?

iii. Who should make the decision, Serena or her parents?

iv. What factors should the decision maker(s) take into account?

v. With whom can Serena and her parents discuss this situation? Should they receive counseling together or should Serena receive counseling alone? ■

E

Whether to Conceive a Child

If you are reading this section first because you are concerned about whether to have a child, we recommend that you turn back to Parts A, B, and C to obtain basic information about genetic testing and insights into the personal and ethical questions it can raise. Then return to this section to look into special issues that can arise when considering conceiving a child.

For those who long to have children, the question of whether voluntarily to remain childless is a painful one made more concrete by our ability to carry out genetic testing. If you learn that any child you conceive would likely have a serious genetic disease, you are bound to ask whether you ought to have children at all. If you have already given birth to a child affected with a serious genetic disorder, you may find yourselves asking, "Should we have others?" This is an agonizingly difficult question to answer. Many who have decided against having children still weep for those they never had.

Where is God in these circumstances? What does God hope for those who face such choices? Do we, as Christians, have an obligation to have children, regardless of the impact of our genes on their health? Or are we called to decide against having children when they might have a condition that would cause them suffering and perhaps premature death? How can our Christian faith guide us in making this decision?

1. Genetics and reasons for considering not having children

a. Why might you ask whether you ought to conceive children?

You may face the question of whether to conceive children because a serious genetic disease runs in your family. Or you may already have given birth to a child with a significant genetic condition and feel concern for any other children you might conceive.

b. How can genetic testing help you decide whether to conceive children?

If you know that members of your family carry a problematic gene, you may wish to be tested to see if you are at risk. A trained professional can test a blood sample from you and one from your spouse to see whether either or both of you carry genes that could lead to a serious genetic condition in your children. When a recessive condition, such as sickle-cell disease, a condition that leads to anemia and a shorter life expectancy, is at issue, tests can reveal whether both members of a couple carry the gene. If they do, their children have a 25 percent risk of having the disease. In this and other instances, it can be difficult to decide whether to conceive children.

Not all genetic conditions, however, have been identified. Thus, while genetic testing can inform you of the likelihood that your children will be born with or will develop a specific genetic condition, it cannot predict every health problem linked to genetics that may arise.

c. How can you learn more about the genetic condition of concern?

If genetic testing indicates that your children are likely to develop a genetic condition, it is important for you to learn about the condition at issue. Many of the factual questions you may have can probably be answered by a physician with special knowledge about genetics or by a genetic counselor. You may want to ask some of the following questions:

- What are the chances that we will pass on a particular genetic condition to our children?
- Can the risk that our children would have this condition be minimized?
- How serious would this condition be? What symptoms do children with this condition have?

- What sources of information about this condition are available to us?

- At what age would the condition appear? How long do children with this condition live?

- What treatments are available for this condition? How difficult are they for children to undergo?

- How expensive are these treatments? Would our insurance cover them? If not, are other sources of financial assistance available for these treatments and other expenses?

- What impact might caring for a child with this condition have on us and our family?

- Would there be sources of social support within our extended family, parish, diocese, or community to help us care for a child with a serious condition?

- If we decide not to conceive a child who is biologically ours, what other options for having children are open to us?

2. Making the decision

a. What choices are open to you if you are told that any child you conceive might have a serious genetic condition?

If you find that you might have a child with a serious genetic disease, there are at least five choices you can make:

- You might decide to proceed with a pregnancy and prepare for the possibility of caring for a child with special needs.

- You might decide to proceed with a pregnancy and prepare for the possibility of ending it should you learn that the embryo or fetus is affected with a serious condition (see below, Part F, section 3).

- You might decide not to have a biologically related child, but to adopt instead.

- You might decide to use artificial insemination of donor sperm or egg with conception initiated by in vitro fertilization (fertilization in a glass dish). (This option raises moral questions that we do not address in this book.)

• You might decide not to have children at all.

b. What does the Christian tradition teach about whether you should have children?

The Christian faith regards bringing children into the world as a joyful act endorsed by God. In the opening chapter of Genesis God tells us to "be fruitful and multiply" (v.28). Having children is one of the purposes of marriage, if it is God's will, the *Book of Common Prayer* declares in the Celebration and Blessing of a Marriage. Yet most Christian theologians maintain that there is no duty for all couples to have children. Although God surely encourages us to have children, the passage from Genesis has not generally been read by Christians to mean that every couple has an obligation to have children. Many Christians believe, for instance, that it is not wrong for those concerned about over-population to refrain from having children and to adopt instead, and that it is morally appropriate for Christians who join religious orders to remain childless. Couples who want to have children, and yet are deeply concerned about the health problems their children might have, may also decide not to have children without moral onus.

A resolution adopted at the 1988 General Convention of the Episcopal Church declared: "Human life should be initiated only advisedly and in full accord with this understanding of the power to conceive and give birth which is bestowed by God." Thus, couples longing to have children, yet concerned about the health problems they may face, must consider whether it is advisable to do so and whether it is God's will.

Some Christians believe that certain illnesses are so severe and so untreatable that we may rightly decide against conceiving children who would suffer from them. Our call to be loving and compassionate people, they believe, means that we have a responsibility not to have children who would face a life of serious incurable illness. Thus, five Christian theologians in the Reformed tradition, which is a cousin of the Anglican tradition, present the following view:

Christians may celebrate and use this new power to diagnose carriers whenever it can result in the avoidance of suffering without doing any harm. To be sure, a decision to forego child-bearing is never an easy one. Moreover, sometimes the decision . . . is a cowardly refusal to take the risk of becoming parents without a guarantee of "the perfect child." But sometimes— when the probability of a genetic condition is high and where the magnitude of the harm caused by the genetic condition is great—the decision not to bear children is a heroic and selfless decision. (Hessel Bouma III, Douglas Diekema, Edward Langerak, Theodore Rotman, and Allen Verhey, *Christian Faith, Health, and Medical Practice* [Grand Rapids: William B. Eerdmans Publishing Co., 1989] p. 255.)

They emphasize that there is no precise mathematical formula for making such agonizing decisions.

Other Christians, however, are concerned that we may have misinformation about the severity of certain genetic conditions and about whether treatment options might be available for them in the near future. Incorrect information may lead us to decide unnecessarily against having children. Moreover, they fear that we may uncritically accept social stereotypes that exaggerate the difficulties of caring for children with special needs. They also are concerned that we may underestimate the resilience of the children, and the support available within the Christian and secular communities. Indeed, both sides agree that the task of deciding whether to conceive a child who would have a serious disease is made more difficult by the social discrimination and stigmatization that children with illness and disability might face. Both sides recognize that we are called, as individuals and as a community of Christians, to work to overcome such discrimination and stereotyping.

c. Would it be wrong for you to decide against having children if you discover that any children you conceive would be seriously ill?

After learning as much as possible about the genetic condition you might transmit, you may conclude that you should not have children. When there is a high probability that you will pass the serious genetic condition to a child and that the condition would cause the child great harm, this decision can be morally appropriate—some would even say a selfless one. If the condition would not be serious, you may want to ask yourself whether you will accept only a "perfect" child, a child with no blemishes whatsoever. In your more realistic moments, you may realize that you can have no such guarantee, given that children may develop a serious condition even after birth. We cannot assume that we will be able to eliminate all difficulties from human life.

If you decide that you should not have a biological child, consider the alternatives open to you and decide whether they might be appropriate for you. This decision is so profound that it is advisable to seek counseling as you make it. Here, too, there are professionals, such as genetic counselors, clergy and other pastoral counselors, psychologists, psychiatrists, and social workers, who can help you through this difficult decision-making process (see above, Part C, section 4).

3. Case for study and discussion about whether to conceive a child

a. Jan's case: Carrier testing for hemophilia and whether to conceive a child

Jan's sister, Felice, has just given birth to a baby boy who has been diagnosed with hemophilia. The blood of those with this condition does not coagulate normally, and they experience excessive bleeding when injured. It is passed from mother to daughter without affecting females. Thus, only males have hemophilia. This new baby is the second child born to one of Jan's sisters to have hemophilia. This suggests that Jan has a one-in-two chance of being a carrier of the gene. Jan and her husband are concerned about whether they should conceive a child.

If Jan undergoes carrier testing for hemophilia and learns that she has the associated gene mutation, that would mean that she has the gene for hemophilia. However, the test is not totally accurate—it picks up only 85 to 90 percent of those who are carriers. Should she test negative and become pregnant, therefore, she could not be sure that she would not have a son with hemophilia. Although she could learn through prenatal testing if she were carrying a male fetus, the testing could not detect whether or not it was affected by hemophilia. Therefore, if Jan and her husband considered an abortion under those circumstances, they would risk aborting a normal male fetus. Finally, Jan has learned that there is a range of severity in hemophilia. Many people with the condition have mild symptoms and those with severe symptoms can be helped by effective, but expensive treatment.

i. Should Jan be tested to learn if she is a carrier of hemophilia? Why or why not?

ii. Should Jan ask Felice or Felice's son to have genetic testing so that she can find out about her own risk and that of her children?

iii. What sort of counseling should they seek? Where can they learn more about hemophilia?

iv. Should Jan and her husband decide to conceive a child? Why or why not? What factors should enter into their decision?

v. If they decide not to conceive a child, should they attempt to have a child in some other way? How? Why?

vi. If Jan becomes pregnant and they learn that she is carrying a male fetus, what should she and her husband do? Why? ■

F

Prenatal Testing

If you are reading this section first because you are concerned about whether to have prenatal testing done, we recommend that you turn back to Parts A, B, and C to obtain basic information about genetic testing and insights into the personal and ethical questions it can raise. Then return to this section to look into special issues that can arise when considering prenatal testing.

As tests become available for an increasing number of gene mutations, they are being offered to more and more people, including pregnant women. It is possible to test a developing fetus to learn whether it has mutated genes or chromosomes associated with certain disorders. "Genetics is changing the process of having a baby," observe Ronald Cole-Turner and Brent Waters, of the United Church of Christ. "What was once a mystery is now rapidly becoming a technologically managed process. Pregnancies are planned, tested, treated, and sometimes terminated for genetic reasons" (Ronald Cole-Turner and Brent Waters, *Pastoral Genetics: Theology and Care at the Beginning of Life* [Cleveland: Pilgrim Press, 1996] p. 14).

As we move from genetic testing before pregnancy to testing during a pregnancy, the moral questions shift radically for some Christians. Does God call us to have children, no matter how ill or disabled they would be? Or does God want us to use the genetic information we have uncovered to avoid bringing children with serious genetic conditions into the world? How can our Christian faith guide us in making such decisions?

Although the decisions we make about having children are intensely personal, they are also deeply social, for they can have an impact on our society's vision of the meaning of procreation and the worth of children. Moreover, such decisions are also religious in that they call on the tradition, guidance, companionship, and consolation of the Christian community.

Many expectant couples proceed with prenatal diagnosis as a matter of course, merely wanting to confirm their belief that their fetus is not affected by a serious condition. At some level, however, they are aware that a problem could be uncovered and that they might consider the possibility of ending the pregnancy. Other couples go through a great deal of soul-searching before they decide whether to undergo prenatal testing. They recognize that they would be grief-stricken should they terminate a pregnancy, and yet they worry that they may not have the spiritual and emotional strength to care for a child with special needs. Both sets of couples cannot help but wait anxiously for the results of prenatal testing.

If you are among them, you may find that you are asking such questions as: Why did we choose to have prenatal testing done? If we receive results indicating that we would have a child with a serious disease, would it be wrong to have an abortion? Would it be wrong not to have an abortion and to have a child who would experience considerable pain and suffering during a life that might be short? Do we have an unrealistic hope of having a "perfect" child? How can we see the tender hand of the creator at work in this situation? Who can help us work through the difficult issues involved?

We offer the following discussion of prenatal testing to those of you who face a pressing decision about whether to employ it and also to those who do not, but who are concerned about the issues it raises. We trust that this exploration of prenatal testing will help you to feel a sense of support from the Christian community, and from the loving God who sustains it and dwells within it, while you are considering this technology.

1. About prenatal testing

a. What is the difference between prenatal diagnosis and prenatal screening?

There are two basic types of prenatal testing. *Prenatal diagnosis* is usually conducted to learn whether a fetus considered at risk of bearing an altered gene for a particular condition actually has that gene. It is also used to diagnose possible chromosomal abnormalities; these involve altered chromosomes, rather than altered genes. *Prenatal screening* is used to evaluate fetuses not known to be at risk to learn whether they might have a mutated gene or a chromosomal abnormality. It also refers to much broader efforts, such as the screening of a particular community or the systematic screening of all newborns. Prenatal diagnosis indicates whether the fetus actually has a mutated gene associated with a genetic condition or else a chromosomal abnormality, whereas screening shows only whether the fetus has an increased chance of having a genetic condition or a chromosomal disorder. If screening suggests that the fetus might be affected, it can be followed by more definitive prenatal diagnostic tests.

Detailed prenatal diagnosis is not done routinely. This is because such tests pose a small medical risk to the fetus and because testing can create unnecessary stress and anxiety for couples who do not have a reasonable chance of having a child with a genetic disease.

b. What sorts of conditions can prenatal diagnosis suggest the fetus might have?

Prenatal diagnosis is usually done to learn whether the fetus has a chromosomal disorder associated with conditions such as Down's syndrome. It can also be used to detect genetic diseases such as Tay-Sachs disease, cystic fibrosis, and sickle-cell disease. Some of these conditions involve substantial functional difficulties, suffering, and early death for the child. Others create certain disabilities in children, but allow them to live a meaningful life for some time. Test results will not always indicate how seriously the child would be affected.

c. Why might you consider having prenatal testing done?

Perhaps you are considering prenatal testing because:

- You or your spouse has a serious genetic condition and you are concerned about whether this might be transmitted to your children.

- You know that a serious genetic disease runs in your or your spouse's family, or a doctor specializing in genetics has told you that your family history suggests that you stand a chance of having a child with a serious genetic disease.

- You or your spouse is known to be a carrier of a gene mutation associated with a genetic condition and you are concerned about whether it might be transmitted to your children.

- You belong to an ethnic group that is at risk for a certain genetic disease and you are concerned about whether it might be transmitted to your children.

- You are a pregnant woman (or her spouse) who may have had several spontaneous abortions in previous pregnancies, suggesting that there may be a chromosomal abnormality involved, and you want to learn whether that is the case in this pregnancy.

- You may have had a screening test that suggests that you have a higher than usual chance of having a pregnancy affected by a genetic problem.

- You have a child with a genetic condition and want to find out whether other children you might have would also have this condition.

- You are a woman of an age at which you are at a higher risk than usual for having children with certain conditions associated with chromosomal changes.

d. What sorts of prenatal tests are there? How are they carried out? What kind of information do they provide?

There are a number of methods used to test for genetic conditions in the fetus. Because of the rapid pace of genetic discovery, genetic tests are revised and updated frequently. We provide here a basic description of most of the tests being used today and recommend that you get more detailed information about them and the conditions they can detect from your physician or genetic counselor.

i. Ultrasound imaging or ultrasonography

This is the prenatal test most commonly used. Sound waves are directed through the pregnant woman's abdomen to enable doctors and technicians to visualize the fetus on a screen. This test does not intrude into the body of the pregnant woman and has no known risk to the fetus. Ultrasonography can be used early in a pregnancy to learn the position of the fetus, estimate its age, assess fetal growth and development, see where the placenta is located, and detect the number of fetuses that are present. Ultrasound imaging can also be used to detect a limited number of possible genetic disorders and certain malformations in the fetus. If its results lead physicians to suspect a disorder in the fetus, other tests can be used to attempt to learn whether this is the case.

Most other prenatal tests available (see below) are more invasive of the woman's body and carry a slight risk of injury to the fetus or of a miscarriage. Furthermore, they require considerable expertise to perform. For these tests, genetic material must be collected and sent to a laboratory, where it is analyzed by a specialist. The laboratory then reports the test results to your doctor.

ii. Amniocentesis

In this procedure a few fetal cells floating in the amniotic fluid are collected through a needle that is inserted through the woman's abdomen into the uterus. These cells are then analyzed for chromosomal abnormalities and for specific genes associated with disease. Amniocentesis is usually performed between the fourteenth and eighteenth week of pregnancy. Because it carries a small risk of injury to the developing fetus and a small risk of miscarriage, it is not routinely used for all pregnant women. It is offered primarily to couples with a family history of genetic disease and for women of an age at which they are at somewhat greater risk of having a child with a chromosomal or other disorder.

iii. Chorionic villus sampling (CVS)

This is another test sometimes used for prenatal diagnosis. It involves inserting a needle through the woman's abdomen and taking fetal cells found in the placenta (rather than in the amniotic fluid surrounding the fetus, as in amniocentesis). These cells are then analyzed for chromosomal abnormalities and specific genes associated with disease. CVS can be performed earlier than amniocentesis, between the tenth and eleventh weeks of pregnancy. There is a debate about whether CVS increases the risk of malformations in the child even if it is done properly. Additionally, this procedure has been found to carry a somewhat higher risk of miscarriage than amniocentesis. Like amniocentesis, this test is not recommended for all pregnant women, but only for couples with a family history of genetic disease and for older women. If a CVS test is positive, health-care professionals may recommend that it be followed by another to confirm the result.

iv. Serum alpha-fetoprotein screening (AFP)

This is another prenatal test, but it is not diagnostic; it does not identify whether the fetus is actually affected with a gene for a given condition. Rather, it indicates that a fetus has a certain chance of having a genetic disorder. Other tests must be used to determine if this is the case. The AFP test is performed on blood taken from the pregnant woman, not from the fetus. Thus, the fetus is not put at risk. The test analyzes protein from the fetus' kidneys that has flowed into the woman's blood. The woman's blood sample is taken between the fifteenth and eighteenth week of pregnancy. AFP testing is used primarily to signal whether a fetus is at risk of having an opening in the spine that could result in harm to the spinal cord and paralysis (as in spina bifida), or abnormal chromosomes associated with certain mental and physical conditions (such as Down's syndrome). If the AFP test indicates an increased risk for such conditions, health-care professionals will usually recommend that the pregnant woman have more detailed testing, often by means of amniocentesis.

Some new prenatal procedures are also being developed and may be available in the future. These include the following.

v. Fetal cell sorting

This involves removing and analyzing fetal cells floating in the pregnant woman's blood. It can be carried out earlier than amniocentesis and CVS, and it does not put the fetus at risk. Fetal cell sorting is expected to be used as an initial test that will need confirmation by amniocentesis or CVS if it should suggest a chromosomal disorder or genetic disease in the fetus. Eventually, medical scientists believe, fetal cell sorting will be used on its own for definitive fetal diagnosis because it involves only a simple blood test. They predict that this test will someday become a standard part of prenatal care for all couples, regardless of their family history or such risk factors as advanced maternal age.

vi. Preimplantation genetic diagnosis

This tests very early embryos for genetic disease, but it is still in the investigational stages. This method can be carried out only on embryos outside of the body through the use of in vitro fertilization (IVF). IVF involves fertilization of eggs from the woman with sperm from the man in a glass dish. A few days after fertilization, when the developing embryo reaches the six-to-eight cell stage, a single cell is removed for analysis, usually without damaging the embryo. (At this stage, the embryo cells are *totipotent*, meaning that each of them can develop into an individual fetus.) This cell can then be analyzed to determine whether it bears the gene for the genetic disease in question. The procedure is carried out on more than one embryo from the same couple because this increases the chances that at least one of the embryos will be free of the disease. Those embryos whose cells are found to have the gene mutation are not used. Those embryos whose cells are unaffected can be transferred to the woman's uterus for further development and birth.

Prenatal tests can be used to test for a variety of conditions associated with specific genes. They are currently used in a minority of pregnancies, but are becoming increasingly common as more and more mutated genes connected with diseases are found and tests are developed that pose less risk to the fetus. Some predict that routine, comprehensive prenatal genetic testing will soon be available to all pregnant women.

2. Making the decision

a. Who should make the decision about whether you should have prenatal diagnosis done?

The responsibility for making the final decision about whether to proceed with this form of testing is yours and your spouse's. This is not an easy decision to make in isolation, and you and your partner may want to share your concerns and feelings about it with those you trust—your family, friends, clergy, and health-care professionals. The suggestions of others can often be of great assistance. Sometimes, however, they can seem more like directives than suggestions, and you may feel pressured to decide in a certain way. Furthermore, because prenatal testing has become more routine and more widely carried out, you may feel social pressure to proceed and believe that you would be out of step with others if you did not have it done.

Yet it is wise not to succumb to such pressure. You should not assume that the decision has already been made by your doctor or family, no matter how well meaning they are. Pause and consider what you think and feel about having prenatal testing done and what you would do with the results. It is important for you to weigh carefully the benefits and burdens of such testing to the fetus, the future child, you, and your family before you decide. It is also important for you to take into account such Christian values as the worth we attribute to children, the commandment to love our neighbor, and our call to prevent great suffering. In the end, it is you who must make the decision, taking all these factors into consideration.

b. What benefits can prenatal diagnosis offer?

A primary benefit of prenatal diagnosis is that it offers reassurance to expectant couples who have it done, because 98 percent of tests carried out show that the fetus does not have a chromosomal abnormality or genetic condition.

Another benefit of prenatal diagnosis is that some couples with a family history of a serious condition who would otherwise remain childless decide to become pregnant because of the availability of prenatal tests. Some of these couples may choose not to proceed with the pregnancy if testing reveals the fetus is affected.

Prenatal testing can also offer a significant benefit to those who have decided against abortion. Should such testing indicate they will have a child with a chromosomal disorder or genetic condition, they can begin to prepare to meet the special needs their child will have.

Some believe that prenatal testing is beneficial because it can identify genetic conditions that can be treated after birth. Unfortunately, few treatments have been developed for genetic conditions. In some cases, a child's diet or lifestyle can be modified to counter the condition, but much still needs to be done to cure genetic disease. Gene therapy, which would alter the genetic material in the cells that express a genetic disease, is at an early stage of development and has not yet had much success. Researchers believe it will eventually prove effective in treating certain genetic diseases, but this will take many more years of development. Treatment of the fetus for certain conditions while it is still in the uterus is under investigation, but this is highly experimental.

c. What are some of the burdens of prenatal diagnosis?

One burden posed by prenatal diagnosis is that some of the invasive techniques currently used for this purpose, such as amniocentesis and chorionic villus sampling, bear a very small chance (1 in 100, or less) of inducing miscarriage.

Further, it can be difficult to predict through prenatal testing the severity of the symptoms associated with certain conditions. Some conditions create very mild symptoms in some children, while in others they exhibit serious impairments that can lead to death. This creates a major problem for couples whose fetus is diagnosed with such a condition, for they cannot be sure how serious their child's condition would be. This variation in the severity of certain conditions makes it difficult to decide whether to consider ending the pregnancy. Moreover, it causes uncertainty in those who choose not to undergo abortion, for they cannot prepare to provide the degree of care their child will need since this is unknown.

Should prenatal testing indicate that a fetus has no diagnosed chromosomal or genetic disorder, this does not guarantee that the child, once born, will be free from disease. This form of testing does not identify many conditions that children may have. Thus, it does not eliminate the burden of uncertainty.

Those who are opposed to abortion under any circumstances believe that a major burden of prenatal testing is that it may lead couples to abort their pregnancy.

Those who are not opposed to abortion find that a significant burden of prenatal testing is the need to wait a few months into a pregnancy until such testing can be done. Many couples find this waiting period emotionally draining. During this time, some women try to ignore the fact that they are pregnant and keep this hidden from others. They do not want to entertain the hope that they might have a child, only to have to abandon it if test results indicate that the fetus is affected and they decide to have an abortion. Barbara Katz Rothman, a sociologist, has termed this the *tentative pregnancy*.

A different sort of burden that prenatal testing presents is noted by several Christian theologians. This burden is not only to us as individuals, but also to us as a community. Prenatal testing, these thinkers believe, can transform the process of having children from a procreative act full of wonder, amazement, and thanksgiving into a more sterile act of production and manufacture. The burden, as they see it, is that as we put greater emphasis on having babies with certain characteristics and who are free of all disability, we run the danger of reducing having children to a form of "quality control," whose goal is to produce "designer children." As prenatal testing increases, children will no longer be thought of as a blessing and a gift, but as objects to be manipulated in ways that fulfill our sometimes distorted views of perfection. Thus, these theologians suggest that we should use prenatal testing cautiously, mindful of our Christian call to respect the dignity of all human beings, regardless of their features or genetic conditions.

d. Is the risk that prenatal testing poses to the fetus greater than the risk of the disease to that fetus?

Some who investigate prenatal testing ask whether it would be unwise to have it done, since some tests bear a very small risk of injuring the fetus, while there is only a slight chance that the fetus will have a serious condition. Though it is true that the odds that a fetus will have a gene for a serious disease are small within the general population, those with a family history of a serious genetic disease have more than a slight chance of transmitting it to their children. These couples are concerned about whether their individual pregnancy is affected and therefore carefully consider whether to have prenatal diagnosis done. Since the risk of testing to the fetus is very small—negligible for ultrasound, 1 in 100 for CVS, and 1 in 200 for amniocentesis—it seems worth taking to some couples whose children have a higher than usual chance of being affected by a genetic condition.

e. To whom can you turn for information and advice as you make a decision about whether to proceed with prenatal testing?

The field of prenatal testing is growing quickly, and your usual sources of support, such as your family and friends, may not have the most up-to-date information about it. Moreover, they may not have given extensive thought to the ethical questions it raises. You might therefore consider turning to knowledgeable individuals in one of several professions, depending on what question is at issue. These include genetic counselors, members of the clergy and other pastoral counselors, psychologists, psychiatrists, and social workers (see above, Part C, section 4)

f. What questions should you discuss with those counseling you while deciding whether to have prenatal diagnosis done?

While we cannot possibly address all the questions that you may have as you make this difficult decision, we offer some that we believe will be helpful for you to take into account.

- Why should we consider having prenatal diagnosis done?

- At what stage of pregnancy are we making the decision about prenatal testing?
- How is the fetus tested? What risks to the fetus does this kind of prenatal diagnosis create? Can these risks be minimized?
- What are the risks of this kind of prenatal testing to the woman?
- How likely is it that the child would have the condition for which testing would be done?
- How serious would this condition be? What symptoms do children with this condition have?
- At what age would the condition appear? How long do children with this condition live?
- How painful and disabling is the condition? How much suffering does it cause to children?
- What treatments are available for this condition? How difficult are they for children to undergo?
- How expensive are these treatments? Would our insurance cover them? If not, are other sources of financial assistance available for these treatments and other expenses?
- If we learn the fetus is affected by a serious condition, what special preparations can we make to care for the child?
- What impact might caring for a child with this condition have on us and our family? Is our family unit stable enough to face the challenges of caring for a child with this condition?
- Are there resources within our parish, diocese, and community to help us and our family care for a seriously ill child?
- What emotional and moral impact might an abortion have on me, my spouse, and my family?
- How can I lessen pressures being put on me and my spouse by family, friends, or health-care professionals to decide one way or the other about having prenatal testing done?

- If we decide not to have prenatal testing done, what problems connected with this pregnancy might we have to face? How can we prepare to address them?

While your primary consideration is the good of the child you might have, your own well-being and that of your family are also very important. It can be difficult to know before a child is born how you might respond as a family. Some families have great difficulty in caring for a very sick child while others have found that they grow closer together as they nurture a child with special needs. This is a matter that you and your spouse will want to consider prayerfully, and perhaps with the help of other family members, friends, and a pastoral counselor.

3. The morality of abortion for genetic reasons

a. Before you can have prenatal diagnosis done, must you agree to have an abortion if results indicate the fetus is at risk of a serious condition?

The accepted belief among medical professionals is that it is the responsibility of patients to decide whether to have an abortion based on their evaluation of information derived from tests and on their religious and moral beliefs. Therefore, most physicians will not require that you agree to terminate the pregnancy should test results indicate that a fetus is affected by a genetic condition.

You should, however, be prepared for the slight possibility that you may have a physician who, before he or she will provide you with prenatal diagnosis, will require you to agree to an abortion should the fetus be seriously affected. Physicians with this requirement feel that it would be wrong for them to be knowingly involved in bringing a child into the world who would experience great illness, as well as pain and suffering. Since couples may have significant reasons for having prenatal testing done, even though they do not plan to have an abortion, as discussed below, this position is indefensible. No physician should attempt to force a woman to have an abortion. If your physician has such a requirement, and if you have chosen not to undergo an abortion should you learn the fetus is at risk of a serious condition, you should find another physician.

b. Should you decide before prenatal testing whether you consider it morally acceptable to have an abortion for genetic reasons? Or should you wait until after?

A decision concerning abortion is a difficult one that is filled with grief and tragedy for many, regardless of the choice they make. Because it is such a momentous decision, it is wise to think through the moral issues involved *before* you decide about whether to have prenatal testing done. This will give you time to reflect about this important moral question in a careful and prayerful way should it arise for you at a later point. If you wait to sort out your beliefs about abortion until after you receive test results, you may be under considerable emotional stress at that time, and may not make as reflective a decision as you would want. You will need to consider whether you believe that abortion is never morally acceptable, whether it can be morally acceptable on certain rare occasions, or whether it can be morally acceptable in a great many circumstances.

c. Who can provide you with sound advice about the morality of abortion for genetic reasons?

While you are trying to decide what is at issue and what you should do, you can talk with your spouse, friends, and clergy about the moral reasons Christian theologians have given for and against abortion for genetic reasons. You may find it helpful to read further on your own to sort through the different theological perspectives that are offered about abortion. Your priest and other clergy can provide you with information, advice, and pastoral support. You will also find it helpful to pray, to ask for the prayers of others, and to continue in the worship and fellowship of the church.

d. What are some basic differences among Christian theologians about abortion for genetic reasons?

Becoming familiar with the reasoning of some Christian theologians regarding the question of abortion for genetic reasons will help you to recognize and understand your own views. You may find that some of their arguments resonate within you and are persuasive. On the other hand, you may find it difficult to relate an abstract theory about the morality of abortion to your concrete circumstances. We offer the following discussion in an effort to equip you with information about the variety of theological approaches to abortion that are held as you sort through the complicated and troubling questions surrounding prenatal testing.

Christian theologians as a whole, and Episcopalians generally, agree that the fetus deserves respect. Consequently, they regard abortion as a morally serious act. They move from this common starting point to express widely diverse views about the morality of abortion.

One major point of difference among theologians and other Christians is about the status of a fetus. Is the fetus a person? If so, it has the same kind of moral standing as those who are born. Some say the fetus is a person from the moment of conception. They therefore believe its life should not be ended because it will have genetic disease. Others maintain that to be a person, one must be self-aware. Since the fetus does not display self-consciousness, they say, it is not owed the protections given to persons. Therefore, they conclude that it is moral to end a pregnancy when testing reveals that the fetus is affected by a serious genetic condition.

Still other theologians say the issue does not revolve around whether the fetus is a person, but whether the fetus is a human being. After all, they argue, newborn babies are not self-aware and yet we believe their lives should be protected. Some among these thinkers hold that the fetus is a human being, and not a chicken or monkey, for instance, from the moment of conception. They maintain that it is a member of our human community regardless of its stage of development and, because it is vulnerable, needs our support. Others say that since cells that are split off from an eight-cell embryo up to fourteen days after conception will each grow into a separate individual, the embryo cannot be considered an individual human being from the moment of conception. Those in this latter group differ about the point at which the fetus has enough of the features of a human being to qualify as one. Some say it is when electrical activity can be found in the fetal brain, providing the initial basis for self-awareness. Others hold that it is when the connection between the brain stem and the neocortex is made between the twenty-first and twenty-fourth week after conception, providing the biological rudiments of thinking and sensing. Still others argue that it is when the fetus has a complete set of human organs and can live outside the womb, for then it is a complete psycho-physical entity with consciousness. When the fetus reaches the stage at which they consider it a human being, these thinkers hold that abortion for genetic reasons would be morally unacceptable.

A second major difference between Protestant theologians who would and those who would not allow abortion for genetic reasons rests in their views of the good of the child who might be born. Those who would allow abortion in some instances hold that whether it is right depends on the severity of the condition the child would have and whether that condition can be treated. If a child would have a serious condition for which there is no therapy and that involves great pain and suffering, these theologians say that it would be morally acceptable to have an abortion for the good of the child. Other Protestant theologians, however, hold that abortion can never be right because life is always a good and a gift from God, no matter how ill and debilitated a person is.

A different but related approach to the question of abortion is taken by Protestant theologian Stanley Hauerwas. He is mindful of our Christian responsibility to create the sort of community in which parents are not forced to care for children with special needs by themselves. Rather than ask, "Is abortion right or wrong?" Hauerwas asks, "What kind of community should we create?" His answer is that it should be one of love and responsiveness to need, one that accepts and welcomes children into the world as a gift. Christians "see children as a sign of the trustworthiness of God's creation . . . ," Hauerwas maintains. Thus, the burning question for Christians should be whether we have the will, as Christians, to develop forms of care and support that would make abortion unnecessary (Stanley Hauerwas, *A Community of Character* [Notre Dame: University of Notre Dame Press, 1981] p. 221). Hauerwas challenges us to make supportive and nurturing communities available to those considering abortion.

e. When prenatal testing indicates the child would have a fatal condition or would never develop consciousness, what do Christian theologians say about the morality of abortion?

Prenatal testing can reveal that a fetus is at risk of a fatal condition. Such conditions can lead to terrible suffering and an early death for the affected child. An example of such a condition is trisomy 18, in which the child has congenital heart disease, difficulty in breathing, other painful physical problems, mental retardation, and an early death. Tay-Sachs disease is another condition that causes severe problems for the child. It affects the child in the first year and involves progressive physical and neurological breakdown before the child dies in about the fifth year.

Prenatal testing can also indicate that a fetus has a severe condition that would leave the resulting child without any consciousness or in a semiconscious state. An example of such a condition is anencephaly, in which part of the brain is missing. The child born with this condition will live without any awareness of others, and with no capacity to know, understand, and relate to others and to God.

Christian theologians reach different conclusions about what action would best serve the good of the child-to-be in these difficult situations. Some Protestant theologians maintain that if prenatal testing reveals that a child would have one of these serious diseases for which there is no treatment, and the child would live only a brief time in pain and suffering, then abortion should be performed for the sake of the child. Abortion is a tragic moral course in these limited circumstances, they believe, but it is the lesser of two evils (David H. Smith, "The Abortion of Defective Fetuses: Some Moral Considerations" in *No Rush to Judgment*, eds. David H. Smith and Linda M. Bernstein [Bloomington:

Indiana University Foundation, 1978] pp. 126-51, and David H. Smith, *Health and Medicine in the Anglican Tradition* [New York: Crossroad, 1986] p. 91).

The Protestant moral theologians of the Reformed tradition cited above have stated this view:

> We recognize the tragedy of a choice among . . . evils, and we can recommend abortion only reluctantly and regretfully, but we do recommend abortion as a course of Christian faithfulness and fidelity in those rare and exceptional cases in which a genetic condition consigns an abbreviated life to such intense pain that life is subjectively comparable to torture, or consigns a brief life to such profound disability that the fetus will never develop God-imaging capacities, even minimally (Hessel Bouma III, Douglas Diekema, Edward Langerak, Theodore Rotman, and Allen Verhey, *Christian Faith, Health, and Medical Practice* [Grand Rapids: William B. Eerdmans Publishing Co., 1989] p. 249).

Other Christian moral theologians would recommend a different course of action in response to these same tragic diseases. Those who view the fetus as a person and who are opposed to abortion for any reason believe that even a short life of serious illness or of semi-consciousness is a good, for life, as a gift from God, is a good. Moreover, all human beings have an inborn worth, and the child who will die soon or be unconscious also has great value they maintain. He or she should be brought into the world to experience love and joy within a family, even if only for a brief time. They would caution others not to accept secular society's standards of personhood, human value, and moral acceptability, which make an easy case for abortion.

In contrast, those who maintain that the fetus is not a person and therefore need not be protected from abortion would allow abortion when a child would be born with a fatal condition or with little or no consciousness, as long as abortion is freely and responsibly chosen. They say that the choice of the expectant couple, particularly of the woman who bears the burden of carrying the fetus, should be the major factor in making a decision about abortion. The burden placed upon the mother, family, and human community at large in making medical, financial, and personal provisions for the care of those born with severe and fatal conditions also weighs heavily in their thinking.

f. When prenatal testing indicates that the child would have a serious condition for which some treatment is available, what do Christian theologians say about the morality of abortion?

In certain other cases, prenatal testing reveals that a child would have a serious condition that is not fatal and whose symptoms could be lessened by treatment. For example, testing may indicate the fetus has the gene mutation connected with a form of colon cancer that occasionally occurs in adolescents (familial adenomatous polyposis). There is no cure for this condition, or any way to prevent it, but removal of the colon can reduce its ill effects and the chance of death significantly. Should parents choose to abort a fetus with this gene?

Some Christian theologians say that when a child would have a serious condition accompanied by great suffering during childhood or later in life, it is morally acceptable to end the pregnancy for the sake of the future child and the family. A loving God, they believe, does not insist that we bring into the world a child who would live in pain and debilitation that cannot be fully alleviated. The family, too, must be considered, for the care of a chronically ill child places a heavy burden on the mother, father, and the community.

Although theologians who disagree with this view can understand that parents would not want to have their children suffer from a serious and painful condition, they believe that parents should not end the lives of these children through abortion. Many people with serious disabilities, they observe, lead meaningful lives, despite the great difficulties they face. Families have been brought closer together through caring for a chronically ill child. Moreover, these theologians suggest that we should not lose sight of the possibility that medical science might devise some means of treating the condition after the child is born, thus relieving his or her suffering.

g. When prenatal testing indicates that the child would have a condition whose degree of severity cannot be predicted, what do Christian theologians say about the morality of abortion?

In still other instances, the degree of severity of a condition diagnosed by prenatal testing cannot be foretold in advance. For example, some children with Down's syndrome, a chromosomal disorder involving mental retardation and sometimes physical disorders, are affected only moderately, whereas others have significant mental retardation and major physical problems. It is impossible to predict how severe the condition would be in a specific child.

Some Christian theologians argue that abortion would be moral in such situations of uncertainty because of the risk of a serious condition in the child. Others state that when the degree of severity is uncertain, abortion should not be carried out because the child might have only a moderate condition. What is at issue here is what weight to give to the degree of risk involved. The first group of Christian thinkers gives greater weight to the risk of a severe illness and opts for abortion, while the second weighs more heavily the possibility of a moderate condition and opts against abortion. Still others believe that it is wrong to engage in such weighing and that regardless of the severity of the condition, a child with such a condition is a valuable human being who should be allowed to receive God's gift of life.

h. When prenatal testing indicates that the child would be at risk of a disease that does not appear until adulthood, what do Christian theologians say about the morality of abortion?

Certain genetic conditions that appear only in adulthood are known as "adult-onset" conditions. These may be included among those conditions for which prenatal diagnosis is carried out in the future. For instance, the gene mutation for Huntington's disease, a rare, fatal condition involving progressive mental and physical deterioration, can be detected in the fetus. When it is found, couples are faced with a terribly difficult question: Should they bring a child into the world who would have this serious, fatal condition as an adult?

This question also arises in families with a history of conditions that, while quite serious, are not as devastating as Huntington's disease and not as certain to occur. For instance, girls in families with a history of a form of breast cancer due to certain gene mutations have a higher chance of developing that cancer as adults. Although female fetuses found to have this gene have a significant chance of developing it later, they will not necessarily do so. Therefore, whether parents should abort the fetus if the gene for this condition is found is a thorny question. Because of the difficulties the child would face later in life, couples with a family history of such diseases may consider ending a pregnancy when tests indicate that their fetus is affected.

There is conscientious disagreement among Christian theologians about what parents should do when tests indicate that a child would have a serious condition in adulthood. Some hold that the moral grounds for abortion in such cases are thin because the child would have many good and meaningful years before the condition at issue strikes—if it does at all. They add that medical science may find a way to treat or even cure many adult-onset conditions by the time the child is old enough to be affected, and they maintain that the child should be brought into the world with this hope. Other theologians, however, hold that the choice belongs to the parents. If they believe that it would be devastating for a child to live knowing that a serious, perhaps fatal, condition might await him or her in adulthood, these thinkers hold that this can provide moral grounds for the parents to choose abortion.

i. **What have Christian theologians said about the morality of selective abortion to avoid having children of a certain sex or of a certain appearance?**

Most Christian theologians find that attempts to choose a child's gender or hair color through use of prenatal diagnosis and selective abortion are wrong in most instances. When there is a family history of a serious gender-linked condition, it can be appropriate to be concerned about the sex of the embryo or fetus because those of one sex will be ill. However, most of these moral thinkers hold that it is not justifiable to abort a fetus with no known genetic disorder solely because a couple does not want a boy or a girl. To do so, they maintain, would be to lose sight of the fact that the child could live a good and satisfying life. Furthermore, most Christian theologians would take the position that, while it is tempting to some of us to want to bring into the world a "perfect" child—what some call a "designer child"—we know in our hearts that this desire is unrealistic and uncharitable. Our children can come with no guarantee of good health, much less good looks. Moreover, while the looks of a child are of esthetic interest, they have nothing to do with the worth of that child. Christians embrace diversity within the human family, and find value in traits that society in general may spurn. There are many differences among us—race, age, height, intelligence, wealth, power—but all of us are of equal significance in ourselves and in our place in the Christian community. What the world regards as weakness, failure, or tragedy, Christ teaches, can bear the image of God. Although a child may encounter social discrimination because of certain physical features, most Christian theologians would argue that this does not justify a decision to abort a fetus before it develops into a child. Instead, we should work toward eliminating such social stereotyping.

j. What does the Episcopal Church teach about abortion for genetic reasons?

You will want to consider statements about abortion for genetic reasons that are set out in resolutions of the General Convention of the Episcopal Church. Such resolutions provide one of several ways in which the Episcopal Church conveys moral teachings on a particular issue to its members. They are meant to assist Christians grappling with difficult moral issues to form their consciences in light of Scripture, tradition, and reason. These resolutions express the reflective thought of bishops and deputies who are knowledgeable about the Church's theological and moral beliefs.

Several General Conventions of the Episcopal Church have passed resolutions concerning abortion for reasons related to genetic testing. In 1967 the General Convention of the Episcopal Church passed a resolution that advocated passing laws that would allow the termination of pregnancy "where there is substantial reason to believe that the child would be born badly deformed in mind or body." A resolution of the 1976 General Convention specifically excluded "abortions for convenience" and reaffirmed support for abortion when the child would be born "badly deformed in mind or body." This resolution urged Episcopalians to seek the advice and counsel of a priest. It was reaffirmed at the next three General Conventions.

In 1988, however, delegates expressed concern that the 1976 resolution implied that all fetuses that might have any sort of genetic condition, severe or moderate, should be aborted. Consequently, a new resolution was passed stating, in part, that:

> All human life is sacred . . . from its inception until death. . . .
>
> We regard abortion as having a tragic dimension, calling for the concern and compassion of all the Christian community.
>
> . . . as Christians we believe strongly that if this right [of a woman to a medically safe abortion] is exercised, it should be used only in extreme situations. We emphatically oppose abortion as a means of birth control, family planning, sex selection, or any reason of mere convenience.
>
> In those cases where an abortion is being considered, members of this Church are urged to seek the dictates of their conscience in prayer, to seek the advice and counsel of members of the Christian community and where appropriate the sacramental life of this Church.
>
> Whenever members of this Church are consulted with regard to a problem pregnancy, they are to explore, with grave seriousness, with the person or persons seeking advice and counsel, as alternatives to abortion, other positive courses of action, including, but not limited to the following possibilities: the parents raising the child; another family member raising the child; making the child available for adoption. (See below, Appendix 2, for the full text of this 1988 resolution).

This resolution, which is the most recent passed by a General Convention, removes the language of the 1976 resolution stating that abortion is morally permissible if "the child would be born badly deformed in mind or body." It advises you to consider abortion only in "extreme situations," but does not detail the nature of such situations. Therefore, in considering the counsel provided in the resolution, you must decide whether yours is one of the "extreme situations" in which abortion would be morally acceptable or whether it fits into those situations in which abortion would be wrong (see David A. Scott, "Changing Teachings on Abortion," in *The Crisis in Moral Teaching in the Episcopal Church*, ed. Timothy Sedgwick and Philip Turner [Harrisburg, PA: Morehouse Publishing, 1992]).

In addition, the 1988 General Convention of the Episcopal Church stated that it is wrong to have an abortion for the purpose of sex selection (see below, Appendix 2).

k. How can you decide about the morality of abortion for genetic reasons, given the diversity of views among Christians?

In reading the brief descriptions above on the different positions of Christian moral theologians and the General Convention resolutions about the morality of abortion for genetic conditions, you have undoubtedly found that there are strong arguments on both sides. Yet, after considering the arguments and conclusions, reading more about the ethical issues and the particular condition of concern, and discussing the question with clergy and laypersons, you may well realize that you have developed a sense that one approach carries greater moral weight than the other. Your touchstones in reaching a conclusion about this difficult matter should be not only your life experiences and deeply felt emotions, but also your prayerful consideration of Scripture, the Christian moral tradition, and your God-given power of reason.

l. If you decide that it would not be morally acceptable to have an abortion, are there any reasons to have prenatal testing done?

There might be reasons for you to have prenatal genetic testing done even if you would not terminate the pregnancy regardless of the information such testing might provide. Should test results indicate that the fetus has a serious condition, you would have time to obtain information about that condition and to prepare for the birth of a child who will need special care. Your planning could include not only emotional and spiritual preparation, but also such practical steps as arranging to have special care available at the time of birth, moving closer to those who can provide you with assistance and support, obtaining insurance, or changing employment. You will find it helpful to discuss these possibilities with your physician, a genetic counselor, a social worker, and other counselors. You may also want to turn to the discussion about caring for a child who has a serious condition (see above, Part D, section 2). Finally, you can consult the list of resources in Appendix 1 and contact those that seem to have relevant information and support systems.

4. Addressing the results of prenatal testing

a. To whom can you turn for information and advice if you learn that the fetus has a chromosomal disorder or a gene associated with a serious condition?

Like most persons grappling with test results indicating that they are carrying a fetus with a serious condition, you may experience emotions ranging from anxiety, shock, guilt, and anger to helplessness and vulnerability. As you decide what to do, you will find it helpful to share your thoughts and feelings with friends and counselors who can offer you empathy and support. You will need reliable information, as well as sound moral advice.

If you have not been in touch with a genetic counselor before this, ask your physician to recommend one. This counselor can help you understand what alternatives are open to you and can point out personal, emotional, and social issues you may want to consider. Talk with a trusted priest or other pastoral counselor about your questions if you have not done so already. He or she can provide pastoral companionship through this time and can let you know that you are not forsaken by God and the Christian community. God's supportive love will be present as you make your decision.

You may want to talk about some of the questions posed above, concerning whether to undergo prenatal diagnosis with others (see section 2f). You may also want to discuss some of the following questions:

- What special needs does a child with this condition have? Would he or she need special schooling or special care in a health-care institution?

- Who would provide the care that the child would need at home? Would family, friends, church and other groups help?

- What special preparations could we make to provide appropriate care for the child?

- How would care of a child with special needs affect our other children?

- How would a decision to have an abortion affect our other children should they learn about it?

- How would we manage financially? Would one of us have to stop working? Would our health insurance cover any of the expenses?

- Are there couples who have a child with this condition to whom we can talk about this?

- Are there others who could care for our child if we can't?

b. Is it wrong for you to feel bewildered and angry with God about these test results?

It is not unusual to feel anger toward God when we learn that we are carrying a fetus with a serious genetic condition. It is natural for you to ask why God has allowed this to happen to you and whether you have done something wrong to deserve this. You may feel that God has let you down or is unfairly punishing you for something you did. You may wonder whether this problem is somehow your fault.

Yet God does not punish us by inflicting serious illness on our children. Genetic conditions develop not because God has decided that specific children will have them, but because of the complexity of genetic processes and their openness to change. We are finite human beings, subject to chance, vulnerable to disease. Yet we can find solace by trusting in God's wisdom as our creator and by knowing that God cares deeply for us and is faithful to us even when we suffer.

c. If you decide to have an abortion for reasons you believe are moral, how can you cope with the grief and emotional pain this will create for you and your family?

A decision to end a pregnancy for genetic reasons can be painful and devastating. Often this is a deeply desired pregnancy that is ended for the sake of the child. Barbara Katz Rothman points out: "It is not the same as an abortion to end an unwanted pregnancy. . . . [Abortions for genetic reasons] mean the loss of a baby. . . . What women told me made this a particularly hard death to bear was that it was profoundly isolating. No one . . . shared their sense of loss" (Barbara Katz Rothman, "Not All That Glitters Is Gold," *Hastings Center Report*, July–August 1992, p. S13).

In their book, *Pastoral Genetics*, theologians Cole-Turner and Waters, raise the hope that God embraces the unborn who are aborted in order to prevent their pain and suffering. They state that:

> We are finding in the resurrection of the body of Jesus Christ a ground for hope of the renewal, not just of ourselves as physical beings, but for the renewal of all creation. . . . We . . . speak coherently of the resurrection of the unborn, the developmentally impaired, the aborted. . . . A God who in Christ makes all things new may in mercy choose to include those who never attain extrauterine life. For just as the God who raised Jesus Christ will transfigure the physical creation which surrounds us like a womb, so God will also transfigure that physical creation inside the womb.

The fetus diagnosed with a serious genetic disorder, they suggest, is joined with Christ in death and resurrection life. The baby that was loved and wanted, they pray, is enfolded into the everlasting arms of God.

d. If you decide, after receiving test results suggesting your child will have a serious condition, not to have an abortion for reasons you believe are moral, could this create social difficulties for you?

Earlier in the twentieth century women became pregnant and had children with little advance knowledge about what the health of their offspring might be. It was considered not only unkind, but completely without justification and nonsensical to fault parents for having a child with a serious hereditary condition. Today, however, it seems that parents are more likely to be blamed for having a child with a genetic condition. What accounts for this? As our ability to test for genetic conditions grows and greater numbers of pregnancies are ended for genetic reasons, others sometimes feel that parents of a child with a genetic condition were negligent in not being tested or foolish in continuing the pregnancy after receiving positive test results. Because their child will require special care from the family and will present additional costs to others in their insurance pool or to taxpayers, critics may believe that the child should not have been born. They may think that these parents should not have imposed on themselves and on society the "burden" of having a child with a serious condition and disabilities.

Consequently, some people with whom you come into contact may isolate and ignore you, feeling that you must accept the consequences of what they view as poor judgment. Others who know you, however, will respect you for making a decision based on what you believe the Christian faith calls you to do. No human being should be regarded as a "mistake" or as "defective," for each of us is precious in the sight of God. Should you find that others blame you for the "sin" of failing to have an abortion when you were aware that you would have a child with a genetic disease, your priest or a pastoral counselor can help you find support from Christians within your religious community.

e. What is eugenics and why are some concerned that prenatal testing might be misused to promote it?

Eugenics is a movement that developed early in this century that sought to improve the human race by controlling human reproduction. People who were considered of "good" quality, according to arbitrary and perverted standards, were encouraged to have children; measures were taken to prevent people deemed of "bad" quality from reproducing. Thus, some who were viewed as "unfit" to be parents were wrongfully sterilized in coercive and discriminatory programs in the United States and Germany in the first half of the twentieth century. Eugenics lost popularity in the United States when it was recognized that such measures violated human rights and dignity. It was developed to an utterly evil extreme, however, in the programs of the Nazis under Hitler. Eugenic sterilization programs have reappeared in other countries around the world more recently. All such programs remind us that humankind has the ability to misuse its medical and genetic knowledge. There comes a point where the legitimate alteration of creation for the benefit of humankind becomes an illegitimate tampering with human beings whom God cherishes.

Some secular and Christian moralists fear that the growing practice of prenatal testing followed by selective abortion could become a contemporary form of eugenics. Individual decisions to abort fetuses who might have disabilities, they believe, could have the cumulative effect of forming a social movement to improve human nature by choosing who should be born. These thinkers predict that by using informal social pressure to weed out fetuses that are "defective" and encouraging couples to deliver only those that are "desirable," we will inadvertently move into eugenics. The wide availability of prenatal diagnosis and selective abortion makes couples who give birth to children with genetic conditions susceptible to hearing others whisper, "They had a child with that condition! What's wrong with them? They could have had an abortion." The possibility of the return to eugenics—in a much more subtle form—hovers over our growing capacities to discover and manipulate human genes.

Some of these secular and Christian thinkers add that the growing use of prenatal testing could lead to objectionable government intrusions into individual procreative decisions and, eventually, to outright coercion. Indeed, they suggest, compulsory programs might be written into laws that require couples to undergo genetic testing and mandate that fetuses that do not have certain approved traits be aborted. Memories of the Nazis are evoked by these thinkers. They recall that the Nazis enacted eugenic laws prohibiting the procreation of "unfit" individuals and stipulating when abortions had to be performed. Could we, too, develop a similar set of eugenic laws?

These thinkers maintain that any move to eliminate or reduce human diversity in the interest of eugenics, or to create a "superior strain" of human being, should be resisted. Such efforts to improve the human race, they point out, would deny the value of all human beings. Other thinkers believe that we would not allow such uses of genetic testing in our civilized society. We are not likely to set aside our morality and Bill of Rights to force couples to have children with socially sanctioned features.

Other Christian moralists have a different focus of concern. They support prenatal testing because it allows us to avoid bringing into the world children who would suffer terribly from serious illnesses. Traditional eugenics programs were morally objectionable because they involved intrusions into reproductive decisions—a private matter—and engaged in outright coercion of their victims. A voluntary decision to undergo prenatal diagnosis and to have an abortion if the fetus would be affected by a serious condition, they maintain, does not amount to eugenics.

f. Why are some concerned that the growing use of prenatal diagnosis and abortion sends an unchristian message to those with disabilities?

Abortion for genetic reasons, some believe, downgrades people with disabilities. Society, in permitting such interventions, seems to be saying to them, "We wish you had never been born." There is a growing concern that the use of prenatal genetic testing will encourage social intolerance of those among us who have genetic conditions or other disabilities. The use of prenatal diagnosis followed by abortion in our society seems to send the message to those with disabilities that we want to get rid of them, these commentators believe.

The response of some secular and Christian thinkers to this is that to prevent the birth of a child with an extremely serious disease does not imply that those with disabilities are not to be valued. Doing so does not say, "We wish you had never been born," but "We wish you had not been born with disabilities." We must distinguish between the person and the condition, affirming the person while attempting to prevent the condition in our children. Yet this is difficult when the disability with which a person is born is linked closely to that person's identity.

Stanley Hauerwas, a Christian theologian, provides a perceptive explanation of the ambivalent and complex attitude of many in our society toward those with conditions that make them different. He says that we want to help them—not to function with their disability—but to be like us. Our inability to do so frustrates and angers us, and we sometimes make those with disabilities the objects of our anger. "We do not like to be reminded of the limits of our power," Hauerwas observes (*Suffering Presence: Theological Reflections on Medicine, the Mentally Handicapped, and the Church*, ed. Stanley Hauerwas [Notre Dame: University of Notre Dame Press, 1986] p. 181). Yet our frustration is uncharitable and unjust. As more and more people come to realize that we all have some gene mutations that put us at risk of having genetic conditions, they will become more accepting of those with serious conditions and more apt to overcome their biases against them. As Christians, we should embrace those with disabilities and set aside any tendency we may have to devalue them. They, like all of us, bear the image of Jesus within them.

5. Cases for study and discussion about prenatal testing

a. Helen and Sam's Case: Prenatal diagnosis for cystic fibrosis

Helen and Sam learn through genetic testing that they each carry the gene for cystic fibrosis. This means that they have a one-in-four chance of conceiving a child with this condition. Cystic fibrosis affects the lungs, pancreas, and sweat glands, and makes breathing and digestion difficult. Helen and Sam's doctor tells them that although great progress has been made in the treatment of this disease, only about half the children born with it survive to become adults. These children require special surgical and medical procedures, as well as physical therapy, exercise, a special diet, and medication.

Helen and Sam have always wanted to have children, and they decide to attempt to conceive one, despite the one-in-four risk of cystic fibrosis. Soon Helen's doctor confirms that she is pregnant. Now they are trying to decide whether to have prenatal diagnosis done. They meet twice with a genetic counselor, who explains how the test is carried out and the sort of information it provides. If the test indicates that the fetus has the mutation for cystic fibrosis, Helen and Sam will have to decide whether they should continue the pregnancy and provide the child with treatment once it is born, or terminate the pregnancy.

The couple is not sure whether to have the test done. At times Helen and Sam think they would rather not know whether the fetus is affected. Yet they ask each other whether it would be right to bring a baby into the world who would experience special physical hardships and probably die relatively early. They wonder whether they could manage the emotional and financial difficulties they would confront if they had a child with cystic fibrosis. On the other hand, they are also troubled by the prospect of an abortion, should the fetus be affected. Could they live with the mixed feelings of grief, relief, anger, and guilt they would undoubtedly have if they ended the pregnancy? They reflect about what they ought to do in light of their Christian commitment.

i. Should they proceed with prenatal diagnosis?

ii. What if they reach different conclusions about what to do? How could they resolve this disagreement?

iii. What would you do if you were in their situation? Have prenatal diagnosis done? And if the test shows that the fetus is affected, have an abortion or carry the fetus to term?

iv. Why? What might you derive from the Christian tradition to help you make this decision?

b. Jane and Bob's case: Prenatal testing and privacy

Jane, who is in the first trimester of pregnancy, learns that she is a carrier of the altered gene for Fragile X syndrome. Although she does not have the disease, she has a 50 percent chance of passing on this gene mutation to her child. Fragile X syndrome is a form of inherited mental retardation that accounts for 3 to 5 percent of those born with a mental impairment.

Jane and her husband, Bob, must decide whether to have prenatal diagnosis to learn if their fetus is affected with this condition. They have always been very private about their difficulties, sharing little with other family members and only occasionally seeking pastoral counseling. Jane has not told her family about this difficult situation.

As they try to make the decision, Jane learns that her younger sister is pregnant. Because Jane is a Fragile X carrier, her sister could be as well, and her fetus also has a 50 percent chance of having the gene mutation.

i. Should Jane have prenatal diagnosis done?

ii. If so, should she and Bob consider ending the pregnancy if they learn that the fetus is affected? Why or why not?

iii. Should Jane tell her sister that she might also have a chance of passing on to her child the gene for Fragile X syndrome? Or should she keep this information to herself and her husband?

iv. Where can they get help in answering some of these questions?

c. Marie and John's case: Prenatal diagnosis for sex selection

Marie and John ask their obstetrician for amniocentesis so that they can learn the sex of the fetus Marie is carrying. They have four girls, ages eighteen months to six years. They desperately want a male child. The couple is not well off, however, and they feel they can afford only one more child. They plan to have an abortion if the fetus is female.

i. Would it be morally acceptable for Marie and John to terminate the pregnancy if the fetus is female? Why or why not?

ii. What factors would you take into consideration if you were in their situation?

d. Georgia and Phil's case: Social discrimination experienced by a couple who decide against abortion

Early in Georgia's pregnancy she and her husband, Phil, learned through sonography that she was carrying twins. When she was seventeen weeks pregnant she had amniocentesis done because she was forty-one years old and therefore had a higher risk for having children with certain chromosomal disorders. Chromosomal analysis revealed that the first twin was normal. The second, however, was found to have trisomy 21, also known as Down's syndrome.

Georgia and Phil knew that children with Down's syndrome are mentally handicapped and are more likely to have certain serious physical conditions, but that they can live happy lives. The degree of illness they might experience, however, cannot be predicted before birth. Georgia and Phil decided that they could not bring themselves to abort the affected twin and have the other. They felt that they would always wonder whether the twin with Down's syndrome could have lived a satisfying life. Furthermore, they were concerned that they might lose both children should they try to remove one. Therefore, Georgia gave birth to the twins, who are now three years old.

When they have needed extra help in caring for the twins, some of their relatives have occasionally assisted them. However, some family members have remarked that Georgia and Phil brought the need for the help of others upon themselves by knowingly having a child with Down's syndrome. Recently, the woman in charge of the three-year-old's group at church asked Georgia and Phil to stop bringing the twins there while they attended the service, for she could not manage a child with Down's syndrome, who needs so much extra care, along with the other children.

i. Did Georgia and Phil have an obligation not to have a child with a chromosomal disorder? Or was their decision to have both children in keeping with their Christian commitments?

ii. What do others owe to couples like Georgia and Phil, who knowingly bring into the world a child who needs special care? ■

Appendixes

Appendix I. Resources

a. General information (arranged alphabetically by organization)

About Face USA Educational pamphlets, booklets, newsletter, videos, and other materials available on facial anomalies, cleft lip/palate, Crouzon disease, Apert syndrome, Treacher-Collins syndrome, hemangioma, and cystic hygroma. Peer support, matching family services, and local chapter referrals offered.
P.O. Box 737, Warrington, PA 18976
(215) 491-0602   1 (800) 225-3223   FAX (215) 491-0603

Alliance of Genetic Support Groups (AGSG) Educational pamphlets, booklets, newsletter and other materials available on genetic conditions. Peer support and matching family services offered.
4301 Connecticut Avenue, N.W., Suite 404, Washington, DC 20008
(202) 966-5557   1 (800) 338-GENE   FAX (202) 966-8553

American Psychological Association (APA) Materials on a variety of psychological subjects, including selecting psychological services and providers, dealing with emotional crises and trauma, and coping with anxiety and depression.
750 First Street, N.E., Washington, DC 20002-4242
(202) 336-5500   1 (800) 964-2000

Association of Birth Defect Children Inc. (ABDC) Educational pamphlets, newsletter, videos, and other materials available on birth defects. Peer support, matching family services, and local chapter referrals offered.
827 Irma Avenue, Orlando, FL 32803
(407) 245-7035   1 (800) 313-2232   FAX (407) 245-7035

Center for Loss in Multiple Birth (CLIMB, Inc.)   Educational pamphlets, newsletter, and other materials available on the loss of one or more children of multiple births at pregnancy, birth, infancy, and childhood. Peer support, matching family services, and local chapter referrals offered.
P.O. Box 1064, Palmer, AK 99645
(907) 746-6123

The Compassionate Friends (TCF)   Educational pamphlets, booklets, newsletter, audiovisual, and other materials available on bereavement and grief. Peer support, matching family services, and local chapter referrals offered.
P.O. Box 3696, Oak Brook, IL 60522-3696
(708) 990-0010   FAX (708) 990-0246

The Craniofacial Foundation of America (CFA)   Educational pamphlets, newsletter, videos, and other materials available on craniofacial anomalies. Peer support, matching family services, and local chapter referrals offered.
975 East Third Street, Chattanooga, TN 37403
(615) 778-9192   1 (800) 418-3223   FAX (615) 778-9011

Family Voices   Educational pamphlets, newsletter, and other materials available on chronic illnesses and chronic disabilities. Peer support, matching family services, and local chapter referrals offered.
P.O. Box 769, Algodones, NM 87001
(505) 876-2368   FAX (505) 867-6517

March of Dimes Birth Defects Foundation   Educational pamphlets, booklets, videos, and other materials available on birth defects. Peer support and local chapter referrals offered.
1275 Mamaroneck Avenue, White Plains, NY 10526
(914) 428-7100   FAX (914) 428-9366

Mental Retardation Association of America, Inc. (MRAA)   Educational pamphlets, booklets, and other materials available on mental retardation and developmental disabilities. Medical referrals offered.
211 East 300 South, Suite 212, Salt Lake City, UT 84111
(801) 328-1574

National Breast Cancer Coalition (NBCC) Educational pamphlets, booklets, and other materials available on breast cancer.
1707 L Street NW, 1060, Washington, DC 20036
(202) 296-7477   FAX (202) 265-6854

National Organization of Episcopalians for Life (NOEL) Affirms within the Episcopal Church and society the sanctity and dignity of all human beings, from conception to natural death. Educational pamphlets, booklets, and other materials available on feasible alternatives to abortion.
405 Frederick Avenue, Sewickley, PA 15143
(800) 707-NOEL   FAX (412) 741-7360

National Organization for Rare Disorders (NORD) Educational pamphlets, booklets, newsletter, and other materials available on rare disorders. Peer support and matching family services offered.
P.O. Box 8923, New Fairfield, CT 06812
(203) 746-6518   1 (800) 999-6673   FAX (203) 746-6481

National Parent Network on Disabilities (NPND) Coalition of parent organizations and parents dealing with general disabilities.
1600 Prince Street, Suite 115, Alexandria, VA 22314
(703) 684-6763   FAX (703) 836-1232

National Parent-To-Parent Network (formerly, Mothers United for Moral Support, Inc.-MUMS) Educational pamphlets, newsletter, and other materials available on rare and general genetic disorders. Peer support, matching family services, and local chapter referrals offered.
150 Custer Court, Green Bay, WI 54301-1243
(414) 336-5333   FAX (414) 339-0995

National Society of Genetic Counselors, Inc. (NSGC) Educational pamphlets, booklets, newsletter, and other materials available on general genetics. Professional counseling referral available.
233 Canterbury Drive, Wallingford, PA 19086-6617
(610) 872-7608   FAX (610) 872-1192

b. Specific conditions (arranged alphabetically by condition)

Alzheimer's Association Educational pamphlets, booklets, newsletter, audiovisual, and other materials available on Alzheimer's disease and dementias. Peer support, matching family services, and local chapter referrals offered.
919 North Michigan Avenue, Suite 1000, Chicago, IL 60611
(312) 335-8700   1 (800) 272-3900   FAX (312) 335-1110

Children, Adults, Attention Deficit Disorder (CHADD)
Educational pamphlets, booklets, newsletter, and other materials available on Attention Deficit Disorder. Peer support and professional counseling referrals offered.
499 NW 70th Avenue, Suite 109, Plantation, FL 33317
(305) 587-3700   1 (800) 233-4050   FAX (305) 587-4559

Autism Society of America Educational booklets, newsletter, audiotapes, and other materials available on autism. Peer support, nonmedical and local chapter referrals offered.
7910 Woodmont Avenue, Bethesda, MD 20814-3015
(301) 657-0881   1 (800) 328-8476   FAX (301) 657-0869

Abiding Hearts Educational pamphlets, booklets, newsletter, and other materials available on birth defects. Peer support, matching family services, and local chapter referrals offered.
P.O. Box 5245, Bozeman, MT 59717
(406) 587-7421   FAX (406) 587-7197

American Cancer Society (ACS) Educational pamphlets, booklets, newsletter, audiovisual, and other materials available on cancer. Peer support, matching family services, professional counseling, and local chapter referrals offered.
1599 Clifton Road, N.E., Atlanta, GA 30329
(404) 320-3333   1 (800) 227-2345   FAX (404) 329-5787

Support Organization for Trisomy 18, 13 & Related Disorders (SOFT) Educational fact sheets, booklets, newsletter, videos, and other materials available on chromosome abnormalities and chromosome anomalies, including Trisomy 13

and Trisomy 18. Peer support, matching family services, professional counseling, and local chapter referrals offered.
2982 South Union Street, Rochester, NY 14624-1926
(716) 594-4621   1 (800) 716-7638

Chromosome Deletion Outreach, Inc. (CDO) Newsletter and other materials available on chromosome deletions, chromosome duplications, translocations, and inversions. Matching family services available.
P.O. Box 280, Driggs, ID 83422
(208) 354-8550

Cleft Palate Foundation (CPF) Educational pamphlets, booklets, and other materials available on cleft palate. Peer support and local chapter referrals offered.
1218 Grandview Avenue, Pittsburgh, PA 15211
(412) 481-1376   1 (800) 242-5338   FAX (412) 481-0847

Cystic Fibrosis Foundation (CFF) Educational pamphlets, booklets, newsletter, and other materials available on cystic fibrosis. Local chapter referrals offered.
6931 Arlington Road, Bethesda, MD 20814
(301) 951-4422   1 (800) 344-4823   FAX (301) 951-6378

American Diabetes Association (ADA) Educational pamphlets, booklets, newsletter, videos, and other materials available on diabetes. Local chapter referrals offered.
1660 Duke Street, Alexandria, VA 22314
(703) 549-1500   1 (800) 232-3472   FAX (703) 549-6995

Association for Children with Down's Syndrome, Inc. (ACDS) Educational curriculum for children with Down's syndrome (ages birth to five years). Pamphlets, booklets, newsletter, audiovisual, and other materials available on Down's syndrome. Peer support, matching family services, and local chapter referrals offered.
2616 Martin Avenue, Bellmore, NY 11710-3169
(516) 221-4700   FAX (516) 221-4311

Little People of America, Inc. (LPA) Educational pamphlets, booklets, newsletter, videos, and other materials available on dwarfism and short stature. Peer support, local chapter referrals, and help with adoption or placement offered.
P.O. Box 9897, Washington, DC 20016
(301) 589-0730   1 (800) 243-9273

Epilepsy Foundation of America (EFA) Educational pamphlets, booklets, newsletter, audiovisual, and other materials available on epilepsy and seizure disorders. Peer support and local chapter referrals offered.
4351 Garden City Drive, Landover, MD 20785
(301) 459-3700   1 (800) 332-1000   FAX (301) 577-2684

Fetal Alcohol Network (FAN) Educational pamphlets, booklets, newsletter, and other materials available on fetal alcohol syndrome. Peer support, matching family services, and local chapter referrals offered.
158 Rosemont Avenue, Coatesville, PA 19320-3727
(610) 384-1133

National Fragile X Foundation Educational pamphlets, booklets, newsletter, videos, and other materials available on Fragile X syndrome. Peer support, matching family services, and local chapter referrals offered.
1441 York Street, Suite 303, Denver, CO 80206
(303) 333-6155   1 (800) 688-8765   FAX (303) 333-4369

National Gaucher Foundation (NGF) Educational pamphlets, booklets, newsletter, videos, and other materials available on Gaucher disease. Peer support, matching family services, and local chapter referrals offered.
11140 Rockville Pike, #350, Rockville, MD 20852
(301) 816-1515   1 (800) 925-8885   FAX (301) 816-1517

American Heart Association Educational pamphlets, booklets, newsletter, and videos available on heart disease.
7272 Greenville Avenue, Dallas, TX 75231-4596
(214) 373-6300   1 (800) 242-8721   FAX (214) 369-3685

National Hemophilia Foundation (HANDI) Educational pamphlets, booklets, newsletter, audiovisual, and other materials available on hemophilia and AIDS/HIV. Peer support and local chapter referrals offered.
110 Greene Street, Room 303, New York, NY 10012
(212) 219-8180 ext. 3049   1 (800) 424-2634
FAX (212) 966-9247

Huntington's Disease Society of America (HDSA) Educational pamphlets, booklets, newsletter, audiovisual, and other materials available on Huntington's disease. Peer support and local chapter referrals offered.
140 West 22nd, 6th Floor, New York, NY 10011-2420
(212) 242-1968   1 (800) 345-4372   FAX (212) 243-2443

Hydrocephalus Association Educational pamphlets, booklets, newsletter, and videos available on hydrocephalus. Peer support and matching family services offered.
870 Market Street, Suite 955, San Francisco, CA 94102
(415) 776-4713

Immune Deficiency Foundation (IDF) Educational pamphlets, booklets, newsletter, and audiotapes available on immune deficiency disorders. Peer support services offered.
25 West Chesapeake Avenue, Suite 206, Towson, MD 21204-4820
(410) 321-6647   1 (800) 296-4433   FAX (410) 321-9165

Polycystic Kidney Research Foundation (IPKR) Educational pamphlets, booklets, and other information.
4901 Main Street, Suite 200, Kansas City, MO 64112-2634
(816) 931-2600   1 (800) 753-2873   FAX (816) 931-8655

Klinefelter's Syndrome Association, Inc. Newsletter and educational audiotapes available on Klinefelter syndrome. Peer support and local chapter referrals offered.
Route 1, Box 93, Pine River, WI 54965
(414) 987-5782

National Marfan Foundation (NMF) Educational pamphlets, booklets, newsletter, videos, and other materials available on Marfan syndrome. Peer support and local chapter referrals offered.
382 Main Street, Port Washington, NY 11050
(516) 883-8712   1 (800) 862-7326   FAX (516) 883-8712

The Arc Educational pamphlets, booklets, newsletter, videos, and other materials available on mental retardation. Local chapter referrals offered.
500 East Border Street, Suite 300, Arlington, TX 76010
(817) 261-6003   1 (800) 433-0553   FAX (817) 277-3491

Muscular Dystrophy Association (MDA) Educational pamphlets, booklets, newsletter, and other materials available on muscular dystrophy and neuromuscular diseases. Local chapter referrals offered.
3300 East Sunrise Drive, Tucson, AZ 85718-3208
(602) 529-2000   FAX (602) 529-5300

National Neurofibromatosis Foundation, Inc. (NNFF) Educational pamphlets, booklets, newsletter, videos, and other materials available on neurofibromatosis (types 1 and 2). Peer support and local chapter referrals offered.
95 Pine Street, 16th Floor, New York, NY 10005
(212) 344-NNFF   1 (800) 323-7938   FAX (212) 747-0004

Osteogenesis Imperfecta Foundation, Inc. (OIF) Educational pamphlets, booklets, newsletter, videos, and other materials available on osteogenesis imperfecta. Peer support offered.
5005 West Laurel Street, Suite 210, Tampa, FL 33607
(813) 282-1161   FAX (813) 287-8214

Sickle Cell Disease Association of America, Inc. (SCDAA) Educational pamphlets, booklets, newsletter, videos, and other materials available on sickle-cell disease, sickle-cell anemia, and sickle-cell trait. Peer support and local chapter referrals offered.
200 Corporate Pointe, #495, Culver City, CA 90230-7633
(310) 216-6363   1 (800) 421-8453   FAX (310) 215-3722

Spina Bifida Association of America (SBAA) Educational pamphlets, booklets, newsletter, audiovisual, and other materials available on spina bifida. Local chapter referrals offered.
4590 MacArthur Boulevard, N.W., #250, Washington, DC 20007-4226
(202) 944-3285   1 (800) 621-3145   FAX (202) 944-3295

National Tay-Sachs & Allied Diseases Association, Inc. (NTSAD) Educational pamphlets, booklets, newsletter, and videos available on Tay-Sachs and forty related conditions. Peer support and matching family services offered.
2001 Beacon Street, Room 204, Brookline, MA 02146
(617) 277-4463   FAX (617) 277-0134

Thalassemia Action Group (TAG) Educational pamphlets, booklets, newsletter, videos, and other materials available on thalassemia (minor, major, and intermediate), beta-thalassemia, and Cooley's anemia. Peer support and matching family services offered.
129-09 26th Avenue, Suite 203, Flushing, NY 11354
(718) 321-2873   1 (800) 522-7222   FAX (718) 321-3340

Turner's Syndrome Society of the United States Educational pamphlets, booklets, newsletter, audiovisual, and other materials available on Turner's syndrome. Peer support, matching family services, and local chapter referrals offered.
15500 Wayzata Boulevard, #811 Twelve Oaks Center, Wayzata, MN 55391
(612) 475-9944   1 (800) 365-9944   FAX (612) 475-9949

If you are interested in another specific support group not listed here, you may contact the Alliance of Genetic Support Groups, which is listed in the general information section, for assistance.

Appendix 2. Relevant Resolutions Adopted by the General Convention of the Episcopal Church

a. Resolutions relevant to genetic testing

Human genetics: Sixty-eighth General Convention of 1985 [A090a]

Resolved, the House of Bishops concurring, That this 68th General Convention encourages genetic engineering research directed to an increase in human understanding of vital processes, recognizing that human DNA is a great gift of God, lying at the center of life and directing our development, growth, and functioning; and be it further

Resolved, That in order to provide effective therapy designed to reduce human suffering, encouragement should be given to the multiplication of "cloned" human genes in especially designed "in vitro" conditions, a process providing the valuable source of pure human proteins which make this therapy possible, provided that through action by Congress authorization is given to the Food and Drug Administration, or to some other appropriate agency which includes those competent in the necessary scientific disciplines and also persons with training in ethics and representatives of the general population and nonscientific members, to assure an ethically acceptable use of these human proteins; and be it further

Resolved, That commendation be given to trained genetic counselors and the organizations which support them; and be it further

Resolved, That the Board for Theological Education and the Council of Seminary Deans be requested (a) to provide for an appropriate group, equipped with pertinent scientific and theological competency, to study the implications of genetic knowledge and genetic manipulation for the Church's teaching; and (b) to include basic training in human genetics in the curricula of our seminary continuing education programs; and (c) to hold up before seminarians and clergy the need for clergy and other ministers to acquire special training in genetics and ethics in order to work progressionally with parents, health professionals, and those caring for babies or other loved ones with genetic disorders.

Guidelines in the area of genetic engineering: Seventieth General Convention of 1991 [A095]

Resolved, the House of Bishops concurring, That the 70th General Convention adopt the following guidelines in the area of genetic engineering:

1. There is no theological or ethical objection against the production and use of medicinal materials by means of genetic manipulation for therapeutic or diagnostic purposes aimed at the prevention or alleviation of human suffering.

2. There is no theological or ethical objection against gene therapy, if proved to be effective without undue risk to the patient and if aimed at prevention or alleviation of serious suffering.

3. The benefits of this new technology should be equally available to all who need these for the prevention or alleviation of serious suffering, regardless of financial status.

4. The use of results of genetic screening of adults, newborns, and the unborn for the purpose of discrimination in employment and insurance is unacceptable.

b. Resolutions adopted by the General Convention of the Episcopal Church relevant to abortion

Abortion: Sixty-seventh General Convention of 1982 [B-9S]

Resolved, the House of Bishops concurring, That the following principles and guidelines adopted by the 65th General Convention (1976) and reaffirmed by the 66th General Convention (1979) be reaffirmed by this 67th General Convention.

1. The beginning of new human life, because it is a gift of the power of God's love for his people, and thereby sacred, should not and must not be undertaken unadvisedly or lightly but in full accordance of the understanding for which the power to conceive and give birth is bestowed by God.

2. Such understanding includes the responsibility for Christians to limit the size of their families and to practice responsible birth control. Such means for moral limitations do not include abortion for convenience.

3. The position of this Church, stated at the 62nd Convention of the Church in Seattle in 1967, which declared support for the "termination of pregnancy" particularly in those cases where "the physical or mental health of the mother is threatened seriously, or where there is substantial reason to believe that the child would be born badly deformed in mind or body, or where the pregnancy has resulted from rape or incest" is reaffirmed. Termination of pregnancy for these reasons is permissible.

4. In those cases where it is firmly and deeply believed by the person or persons concerned that pregnancy should be terminated for causes other than the above, members of this Church are urged to seek the advice and counsel of a Priest of the Church, and, where appropriate, penance.

5. Whenever members of this Church are consulted with regard to proposed termination of pregnancy, they are to explore, with the person or persons seeking advice and counsel, other preferable courses of action.

Gender Selection: Sixty-seventh General Convention of 1982 [A-65a]

Whereas, new biomedical diagnostic techniques now allow the detection of a wide range of medical abnormalities in the unborn child; and

Whereas, the gender of the prospective newborn can also be determined by the same techniques; and

Whereas, such information gives rise to the need for serious and difficult decisions of continuing a pregnancy; therefore be it

Resolved, the House of Bishops concurring, That the 67th General Convention of the Episcopal Church strongly condemns the act of abortion when the sole purpose of such action is the selection of the sex of the child; and be it further

Resolved, That this new ability to diagnose serious abnormalities in the fetus before birth is a welcome gift to reduce pain and sorrow in the parents and suffering in the newborn, but that abortion after the diagnosis of nonserious or trivial abnormalities, or abortion in a case where purely cosmetic abnormalities are discovered, is also strongly condemned.

Adopt a statement on childbirth and abortion: Sixty-ninth General Convention of 1988 [C047]

Resolved, the House of Deputies concurring, That the 69th General Convention adopt the following statement on childbirth and abortion:

All human life is sacred. Hence, it is sacred from its inception until death. The Church takes seriously its obligation to help form the consciences of its members concerning this sacredness. Human life, therefore, should be initiated only advisedly and in full accord with this understanding of the power to conceive and give birth which is bestowed by God.

It is the responsibility of our congregations to assist their members in becoming informed concerning the spiritual and physiological aspects of sex and sexuality.

The *Book of Common Prayer* affirms that "the birth of a child is a joyous and solemn occasion in the life of a family. It is also an occasion for rejoicing in the Christian community" (p. 440). As Christians we also affirm responsible family planning.

We regard all abortion as having a tragic dimension, calling for the concern and compassion of all the Christian community.

While we acknowledge that in this country it is the legal right of every woman to have a medically safe abortion, as Christians we believe strongly that if this right is exercised, it should be used only in extreme situations. We emphatically oppose abortion as a means of birth control, family planning, sex selection, or any reason of mere convenience.

In those cases where an abortion is being considered, members of this Church are urged to seek the dictates of their conscience in prayer, to seek the advice and counsel of members of the Christian community and where appropriate, the sacramental life of this Church.

Wherever members of this Church are consulted with regard to a problem pregnancy, they are to explore, with grave seriousness, with the person or persons seeking advice and counsel, as alternatives to abortion, other positive courses of action including, but not limited to, the following possibilities: the parents raising the child; another family member raising the child; making the child available for adoption.

It is the responsibility of members of this Church, especially the clergy, to become aware of local agencies and resources which will assist those faced with problem pregnancies.

We believe that legislation concerning abortions will not address the root of the problem. We therefore express our deep conviction that any proposed legislation on the part of national or state governments regarding abortions must take special care to see that the individual conscience is respected, and that the responsibility of individuals to reach informed decisions on this matter is acknowledged and honored.

Abortion: Seventy-first General Convention of 1994 [A054s]

Resolved, the House of Bishops concurring, That this 71st General Convention of the Episcopal Church reaffirms Resolution C047 from the 69th General Convention, which states:

All human life is sacred. Hence, it is sacred from its inception until death. The Church takes seriously its obligation to help form the consciences of its members concerning this sacredness. Human life, therefore, should be initiated only advisedly and in full accord with this understanding of the power to conceive and give birth which is bestowed by God.

It is the responsibility of our congregations to assist their members in becoming informed concerning the spiritual and physiological aspects of sex and sexuality.

The *Book of Common Prayer* affirms that "the birth of a child is a joyous and solemn occasion in the life of a family. It is also an occasion for rejoicing in the Christian community" (p. 440). As Christians we also affirm responsible family planning.

We regard all abortion as having a tragic dimension, calling for the concern and compassion of all the Christian community.

While we acknowledge that in this country it is the legal right of every woman to have a medically safe abortion, as Christians we believe strongly that if this right is exercised, it should be used only in extreme situations. We emphatically oppose abortion as a means of birth control, family planning, sex selection, or any reason of mere convenience.

In those cases where an abortion is being considered, members of this Church are urged to seek the dictates of their conscience in prayer, to seek the advice and counsel of members of the Christian community and where appropriate, the sacramental life of this Church.

Wherever members of this Church are consulted with regard to a problem pregnancy, they are to explore, with grave seriousness, with the person or persons seeking advice and counsel, as alternatives to abortion, other positive courses of action including, but not limited to, the following possibilities: the parents raising the child; another family member raising the child; making the child available for adoption.

It is the responsibility of members of this Church, especially the clergy, to become aware of local agencies and resources which will assist those faced with problem pregnancies.

We believe that legislation concerning abortions will not address the root of the problem.

We therefore express our deep conviction that any proposed legislation on the part of national or state governments regarding abortions must take special care to see that the individual conscience is respected, and that the responsibility of individuals to reach informed decisions on this matter is acknowledged and honored as the position of this Church; and be it further

Resolved, That this 71st General Convention of the Episcopal Church expresses its unequivocal opposition to any legislative, executive, or judicial action on the part of local, state, or national governments that abridges the right of a woman to reach an informed decision about the termination of pregnancy or that would limit the access of a woman to safe means of acting on her decision. ■

Bibliography

Ames, David A., and Colin B. Gracey, eds. *Good Genes? Emerging Values for Science, Religion and Society.* Cincinnati: Forward Movement, 1984.

Andrews, Lori B., Jane E. Fullarton, Neil A. Holtzman, and Arno G. Motulsky, eds. *Assessing Genetic Risks: Implications for Health and Social Policy.* Washington, DC: National Academy Press, 1994.

Biesecker, B.B., M. Boehnke, K. Calzone, D. S. Market, J. E. Garber, F. S. Collins, and B. L. Weber. "Genetic Counseling for Families with Inherited Susceptibility to Breast and Ovarian Cancer." *Journal of the American Medical Association* 269 (1993): 1970–74.

Bouma III, Hessel, Douglas Diekema, Edward Langerak, Theodore Rotman, and Allen Verhey. *Christian Faith, Health, and Medical Practice.* Grand Rapids: William B. Eerdmans Publishing Co, 1989.

Cohen, Cynthia B. "Wrestling with the Future: Predictive Genetic Testing of Children." *Kennedy Institute of Ethics Journal* 8 (1998): 111–30.

Cole-Turner, Ronald. *The New Genesis: Theology and the Genetic Revolution.* Louisville: Westminster John Knox, 1993.

Cole-Turner, Ronald, and Brent Waters. *Pastoral Genetics: Theology and Care at the Beginning of Life.* Cleveland: Pilgrim Press, 1996.

Collins, Francis F. "BRCA1—Lots of Mutations, Lots of Dilemmas." *New England Journal of Medicine* 334 (1996): 186–88.

Fletcher, John C. *Coping with Genetic Disorders: A Guide for Clergy and Parents.* New York: Harper and Row, 1982.

Habgood, John. "An Anglican View of the Four Principles." In *Principles of Health Care Ethics.* Edited by Raanan Gillon. London: John Wiley & Sons, 1994, pp. 55–64.

Hauerwas, Stanley. *A Community of Character.* Notre Dame, IN.: Notre Dame Press, 1981.

Hauerwas, Stanley. *Suffering Presence: Theological Reflections on Medicine, the Mentally Handicapped, and the Church.* Notre Dame, IN: University of Notre Dame Press, 1986.

Kelves, Daniel J. *In the Name of Eugenics: Genetics and the Uses of Human Heredity.* Berkeley, CA: University of California Press, 1985.

Kristol, Elizabeth. "Picture Perfect: The Politics of Prenatal Testing." *First Things* 32 (1993): 17.

Lebacqz, Karen. ed. *Genetics, Ethics and Parenthood.* New York: Pilgrim Press, 1983.

Lewis, C.S. *The Abolition of Man.* New York: Macmillan, 1947.

Lippman, Abby. "The Genetic Construction of Testing: Choice, Consent, or Conformity for Women." In *Women and Prenatal Testing: Facing the Challenges of Genetic Testing.* Edited by Karen H. Rothenberg and Elizabeth J. Thomson. Columbus: Ohio State University Press, 1994, 9–34.

Nelkin, Dorothy, and Laurence Tancredi. *Dangerous Diagnostics: The Social Power of Biological Information.* New York: Basic Books, 1989.

O'Donovan, Oliver. *Begotten or Made?* Oxford, England: Clarendon Press, 1984.

Peacocke, Arthur. *God and the New Biology.* London: Dent, 1986.

Peacocke, Arthur. *Theology for a Scientific Age: Being and Becoming—Natural, Divine and Human.* Minneapolis: Fortress Press, 1993.

Peters, Ted. "Designer Children: The Market World of Reproductive Choice." *Christian Century* 14 (1994): 1196–2002.

Polkinghorne, John C. *One World.* Princeton, NJ: Princeton University Press, 1986.

Post, Stephen G. "Designer Babies, Selective Abortion, and Human Perfection." In *Inquiries in Bioethics by Stephen G. Post.* Washington, DC: Georgetown, 1993, pp. 7–21.

Ramsey, Paul. *Fabricated Man: The Ethics of Genetic Control.* New Haven, CT.: Yale University Press, 1970.

Rothman, Barbara Katz. "Not All That Glitters Is Gold." *Hastings Center Report* (1992): S12–13.

Rothman, Barbara Katz. "The Tentative Pregnancy: Then and Now." In *Women and Prenatal Testing: Facing the Challenges of Genetic Testing*. Edited by Karen H. Rothenberg and Elizabeth J. Thomson. Columbus: Ohio State University Press, 1994, pp. 9–34.

Smith, David H., Kimberly A. Quaid, Roger B. Dworkin, Gregory P. Gramelspacher, Judith A. Granbois, and Gail H. Vance. *Early Warning: Cases and Ethical Guidance for Presymptomatic Testing in Genetic Diseases*. Bloomington: Indiana University Press, 1998.

Stephenson, Joan. "Questions on Genetic Testing Services." *Journal of the American Medical Association* 274 (1995): 1661–62.

Wertz, Dorothy, Joanna Fanos, Philip R. Reilly. "Genetic Testing for Children and Adolescents." *Journal of the American Medical Association* 272 (1994): 875–81.

Working Party of the Clinical Genetics Society. "The Genetic Testing of Children." *Journal of Medical Genetics* 31 (1994): 785–97. ∎

Committee Members
Who Developed This Report

The Rev. Joan Beilstein, M. Div., is interim rector at the Church of the Nativity, Camp Springs, Maryland, and Director of Pastoral Care and chaplain at Manor Care Health Services. She is a member of the ethics committee at Manor Care, Fair Oaks. The Rev. Beilstein has provided pastoral care and counseling at several health-care institutions.

Barbara Bowles Biesecker, M.S.,* is genetic counselor and co-director of the Genetic Counseling Research and Training Program in the Medical Genetics Branch of the National Human Genome Research Institute at the National Institutes of Health, Bethesda, Maryland. She has served as president of the National Society of Genetic Counselors. Her areas of interest include research in genetic counseling, psychological ramifications of genetic conditions, and implications of genetic testing, particularly for predictive cancer risk.

Cynthia B. Cohen, Ph.D., J.D., is chair of the Committee on Medical Ethics of the Episcopal Diocese of Washington, a Senior Research Fellow at the Kennedy Institute of Ethics at Georgetown University, Washington, DC, and Adjunct Associate at The Hastings Center in Garrison, New York. She has authored books and articles on ethical issues related to the beginning and end of life. She also serves on the Stand-

---

*Ms. Biesecker and Dr. DeRenzo participated in the development of this book in their private capacity. No official support or endorsement by the National Institutes of Health, any other Federal agency, or any other institution or organization with which they are affiliated is intended or should be inferred.

ing Commission on National Concerns of the Protestant Episcopal Church and chairs its End-of-Life Task Force.

The Rt. Rev. Theodore Daniels, M. Div., is bishop of the Diocese of the Virgin Islands, and is also a trained pastoral psychotherapist. He currently serves as a member of the Standing Commission on International and Anglican Peace with Justice Concerns. He is the former president of the Episcopal Clergy Association of the Diocese of Washington and former chair of the Christian Education Committee of the diocese.

Evan Gaines DeRenzo, Ph.D.,* is senior staff fellow in the Department of Clinical Bioethics at the National Institutes of Health and adjunct faculty at The Johns Hopkins University and Marymount University in Virginia. Her present research activities focus on ethical issues raised by involving cognitively and psychiatrically impaired persons in research, as well as on ethical issues in oncology, genetics, and other aspects of biotechnology.

Peggy Eastman is a medical and science writer who has written extensively about genetic susceptibility to cancer in *Oncology Times*, for which she serves as Washington contributing writer. She has also written about genetics for *Cardiology World News* and *AARP Bulletin* (published by the American Association of Retired Persons). Author of the book, *Your Child Is Smarter Than You Think*, she has written for many national publications.

Wendy J. Fibison, Ph.D., M.H.Sc., P.N.P., conducts research in the Clinical Gene Therapy Branch of the National Center for Human Genome Research Institute as a recipient of an Intramural Research Training Award sponsored by that Institute and the National Institute of Nursing Research, National Institutes of Health. The focus of her work is on single-cell analysis of clinical gene therapy and ethical issues related to genetic therapy and genetic testing.

Carol Lee Hilewick, M.A., Ph.D., DACFE, DABFM, is a psychologist in private practice in Kensington, Maryland. She assesses and treats individuals with chronic or terminal illnesses, temporary or permanent disabilities, pain, and trauma. She treats individuals suffering from serious mental illness and personality disorders. She consults on bioethical issues in medical and psychological treatment, in particular, on iatrogenic harm, confidentiality, and informed consent.

Noel Anketell Kramer, J.D., has been a judge on the Superior Court for the District of Columbia for the past thirteen years. She has ruled on issues concerning medical care for minors and incapacitated individuals, and anticipates confronting in the future multiple issues arising from genetic testing. She has also been involved in drafting the Code of Judicial Conduct for the DC courts and other areas of legal ethics.

Elizabeth Luck, M.D., M.T.S., is a neurosurgeon who has also done graduate work in theological studies, with a special emphasis on medical ethics, at the Virginia Theological Seminary.

James H. Marchbank is the director of finance and administration for the Rock Creek International School in Washington, DC. He served as administrator for a special-education school for eight years, and has also had extensive experience in hospital, home health, and clinic settings. His interests in genetic testing are in preventing genetic conditions and in providing families with the support and knowledge they need to make decisions when they know they may bring a severely handicapped child into the world.

James L. Mills, M.D., Ph.D., is a pediatrician and epidemiologist who carries out research on birth defects. His particular interests include nutrition and diabetes as factors in the etiology of birth impairments.

Judith W. Smith, Ph.D., is an historian who has served as an associate editor of a scholarly journal and has taught at several colleges and universities in the United States and overseas. She has authored a number of essays on historical topics and has a long-standing interest in the history of science and in bioethics.

Karen Roberts Turner, M.A., J.D., is a litigation associate in the Washington, DC law firm of Montedonico, Hamilton, and Altman. She specializes in medical malpractice and insurance defense. Ms. Turner has worked as a clinical ethicist at the Washington Hospital Center and is an assistant professor of health-care ethics at the Howard University College of Medicine. ■